CW00616614

BUILT

BUILT TO LAST?

Reflections on British housing policy

Edited by Carol Grant

First published in 1992 by ROOF Magazine, Shelter, 88 Old Street, London
EC1V 9HU.

© ROOF magazine

British Library Cataloguing in Publication Data
Built to Last? Reflections on British Housing Policy
A Collection of Articles from ROOF Magazine
   I. Grant, Carol
   363.50941
   ISBN 1-870767-11-X

Typesetting, page make up and print by The Russell Press, Radford Mill,
Norton Street, Nottingham NG7 3HN.

Cover photo: Houses in Noel Road, Islington, reflected in the Regents Canal,
North London, by Jon Walter.

Acknowledgements

This book could not have been produced without the time, energy and enthusiasm of its many contributors, listed overleaf. Thanks are also due to Peter Malpass, who had the original idea for the book, and who, as well as contributing three chapters, also indexed the collection of articles. Peter Williams, as well as writing a new concluding chapter, also gave much useful advice on the book's format and style.

The original articles were sub-edited by ROOF staff, retyped by Mary Farrugia and proofread by David Morgan. Picture research was by Tim Dwelly.

Contributors

Ron Bailey is a campaigner on squatting and empty property.

Martin Boddy is Reader in Land and Development Studies at the School for Advanced Urban Studies in Bristol.

David Clapham is Senior Research Fellow at the Centre for Housing Research in Glasgow.

Seán Damer is a freelance writer and formerly worked at the Centre for Housing Research in Glasgow.

John English is a Lecturer at the University of Paisley.

Ray Forrest is Reader in Advanced Urban Studies at the School for Advanced Urban Studies in Bristol.

Pat Garside is Senior Lecturer in the Department of Environmental Health and Housing at the University of Salford.

Sara Hill is a Research Associate in the Department of Geography at the University of Edinburgh.

Peter Kemp is Joseph Rowntree Professor of Housing and Director of the Centre for Housing Policy at the University of York.

Peter Malpass is Professor of Housing Policy at the University of the West of England, Bristol.

Contributors

Robin Means is Lecturer in Advanced Urban Studies at the School for Advanced Urban Studies in Bristol.

Alan Murie is Professor of Planning and Housing at Edinburgh College of Art.

Martin Pawley is Editor of World Architecture Magazine and was formerly architecture correspondent for The Guardian.

Janet Richards is Principal Policy Officer (Tenant Services) at the Institute of Housing.

Susan Smith is Professor of Geography at the University of Edinburgh.

Paul Spicker is a Lecturer in Social Policy at the University of Dundee.

Jerry White works in local government in London.

Peter Williams is Professor of Housing Management at the Centre for Housing Management and Development at the University of Wales College of Cardiff.

Contents

Foreword

ROOF's Second Take series was conceived in 1988, at a time when the proposals in the government's 1987 White Paper on housing were being put into practice. It was a time of a major shift in direction for housing policy. Councils were sidelined as providers of social housing, and housing associations were given the job of filling a very large gap in provision. The private rented sector was being deregulated, and key changes to the financial arrangements for social housing were being formulated.

Outside the housing arena, the changes in local government finance which resulted in the poll tax focused attention on local government's autonomy and the role of local communities in resisting unpopular measures.

ROOF is an editorially independent housing magazine published by Shelter. Its strength has always been to put housing policy into a social, political and economic context, to challenge existing orthodoxies, and to develop new ideas and directions. What better way to allow readers to make their own critical judgements about current policies than to locate them in an historical continuum?

The shelves are stacked with books on housing history. When we began the Second Take series in ROOF, we wanted to avoid an overly academic approach to a living subject, even though many of our contributors were respected housing academics. The challenge for them was to produce readable pieces of social history that had relevance to today's housing practioners, students, and general readers. This book's publication, with many of the original articles expanded and updated, is

testimony to how successfully the contributors met that
challenge.

Some of the chapters are, by their nature, quite detailed. To
understand why policies have developed on how housing should
be paid for, one has to follow complicated trends in deficit
subsidies, rebate schemes and the rest. But housing is about
people, and our contributors to the Second Take series have
populated their articles not just with the hard facts and figures,
but also with the people whose experiences shaped the outcome
of housing policy.

Housing finance may seem a dry subject, but no-one could
read about the struggle of the Glasgow rent strikers (which had
such a fundamental effect on the financing of private rented
housing) or the fight of the Clay Cross councillors over the
principle of local autonomy on rent setting, without
appreciating how individuals at a local level, as well as senior
policy makers, have influenced the housing system we have
inherited.

This book is designed to inform, to entertain, and to stimulate
those interested in housing to think about how their current
views, practices, and the policies they may have to implement,
have been shaped by earlier generations.

Although these articles were prompted by the seemingly
radical changes to housing policy being proposed in 1987,
perhaps the judgement, after reading this book, will be that
there is nothing new under the sun. Homelessness, the relative
merits of owning or renting, the motivation for investors and
builders to provide new homes, the cost of housing, patterns
of discrimination — all these current issues have their roots in
the past.

To develop and implement housing policies that work, and
that meet diverse housing needs in a way that is cost-effective,
efficient and satisfies modern standards and aspirations, we
have to build our policies on a firm foundation of knowledge.
Only then will Britain have a housing policy that can truly be
said to be built to last.

Carol Grant
Editor
ROOF magazine

Chapter 1

Business out of charity

Were the early charitable housing trusts a philanthropic response to housing need, or a hard headed use of capital to quell working class unrest?

Jerry White

Housing associations have their origins in the 1840s, that troubled decade of famine in Ireland and 'the hungry forties' in the rest of Britain; of revolutions across Europe and Chartism and riot at home, with hastily-armed volunteers patrolling the Bank of England to protect it from popular pillage.

The appearance of the housing association movement at that turbulent time was no accident. The beginnings of housing associations are deeply rooted in class relations and in the nature and function of the British state. The shadows cast by those origins remain plainly visible today.

The middle class public of the 1840s was bombarded as never before by information, both reportage and statistics, on working class living conditions. Public health reports, newspaper 'special correspondents' and novelists all provided detailed and sometimes lurid exposure of Liverpool cellars, stilt dwellings in Bermondsey's Jacob's Island, dung heaps as high as houses in Bethnal Green, Glasgow 'wynds' and courts so narrow you could touch the high buildings on either side by stretching out your arms. Drainage, water supply and sanitary dwellings became the urgent concern of middle class reformers and the new local government structures organised around public health.

Pity for the poor undoubtedly spurred on rich men and women to do something to remedy the conditions they read about. The first housing association is said to have been the Metropolitan Association for Improving the Dwellings of the Industrious Classes, formed in 1841, but not building actively until a few years later. The busiest of the first associations, the Society for Improving the Conditions of the Labouring Classes (1844), was part-founded by the Earl of Shaftesbury, an evangelical christian and tireless social reformer. Prince Albert, not the last royal with an interest in housing reform, became its president, and its first tenement dwellings were built in Gray's Inn Road, London, for 50 households, 30 of them single people. One of the Society's first ventures, in Bloomsbury, still stands as a monument to the humanitarian ideals of the very first housing associations.

The 1860s saw the flowering of the housing association movement with City alderman (later Sir) Sydney Waterlow's dwellings in Finsbury, followed by his formation of the Improved Industrial Dwellings Company; and by the donation by the American merchant George Peabody of £150,000 (rising to £500,000) to the poor of London in 1862.

Peabody's gift — which was to be a thorn in the side of the capitalists who saw housing associations as a business — was the single greatest act of charity of his day. The Peabody and Waterlow tenement block dwellings were to help change the face of London's old City suburbs of Finsbury, Shoreditch, Bethnal Green, Southwark, Holborn and Westminster over the next 40 years.

In the face of such munificence it might seem carping to remember that humanitarianism does not exclude self-interest. And it is clear that, from the very earliest days, bourgeois philanthropy expressed through the housing association movement was rarely disinterested. Housing associations were seen to benefit the middle classes too; not, of course, by providing cheap dwellings for them, but in the social benefits which improvement in working class living conditions brought.

Housing reform was seen as a cure for crime in areas like Spitalfields, where churchgoers needed police protection from

Joseph Rowntree Foundation

Parlour in house in New Earswick, Joseph Rowntree's model village in York.

bag-snatchers and 'hooligans'; for pauperism through drink and other causes; for infectious diseases like cholera and smallpox which would not recognise the boundaries between poor and prosperous neighbourhoods; and for political unrest. 'Ay, truly,' Shaftesbury enthused after a meeting to publicise the work of his Society in 1848, 'this is the way to stifle Chartism.' And this explicit political purpose was no doubt prominent in the minds of philanthropic employers who devised model villages for their workers, like Salt, Cadbury, Rowntree, Akroyd and others in the 1850s and 1860s.

Capitalist speculation in working class housing had, of course, a long history but also, by the 1840s, a bad reputation. Landlords were exposed as house-screwers, house-jobbers, rackrenters and slumlords in the 1840s, as they were to be again by the Royal Commission on the Housing of the Working Classes in 1885. But from the earliest days, some housing associations were consciously seeking to make capital investment in working class housing respectable.

This aspect of the movement has often been called semi-philanthropic and the name is well chosen. There undoubtedly was a charitable element in choosing this way to invest money rather than, say, railways, imperial ventures, or slum property. But the investment opportunities offered by the associations were not insignificant. The Metropolitan Association of 1841 was set up on these 'strict business principles' to yield five per cent per annum on capital invested — not a bad return in those less usurious times. And in the years to follow, a good number of associations took this road — explicitly capitalist, but with charitable hedgerows.

Waterlow's company in the 1860s eventually raised £500,000 capital, after considerable mistrust from investors who did not believe a charitable enterprise could be made to pay. It was followed by the Artisans', Labourers', and General Dwellings Company, formed in 1867 and specialising in cottage estates. But the main era of the semi-philanthropic housing associations was the 1880s, with a fresh rediscovery of the housing problem and renewed fears of political unrest, especially in London. The East End Dwellings Company, the Four Per Cent Industrial Dwellings Company, and the Guinness Trust were the biggest semi-philanthropic associations to emerge in that decade.

The 1880s also revealed the tensions within the movement between the charitable organisations, represented pre-eminently by Peabody, and those on the capitalist road. Arguments arose particularly over the state-inspired disposal of slum clearance sites in central London. The semi-philanthropists claimed that Peabody, without investors' interests to safeguard, could afford to outbid other companies for the best sites; and they could afford to build to higher standards, attracting those tenants — policemen, clerks, railwaymen — best able to pay. This was one reason why investors were hard to come by and why the greatest problem of the semi-philanthropic associations was shortage of capital. In the final outcome, private investment was inadequate to solve the working class housing problem, even with the state playing the role of enabler.

Until 1919, the British state consciously stood back from the working class housing problem. A post-war period of considerable unrest provoked a definitive interventionist response which was to characterise housing policy until 1980.

But the role of the state before the First World War had stopped well short of public housing provision. Although the Housing of the Working Classes Act 1890 had allowed for rate-borne building by local authorities, only a few took the opportunity. Prior to that, councils were stopped from building for rent. When they cleared slums they had to dispose of the assembled sites to a developer who would build working class housing on them: the role of developer in this context was adopted by the housing associations — both capitalist and charitable wings.

The key piece of legislation which enabled housing associations to play this role was the Artisans' and Labourers' Dwellings Improvement Act 1875 — known as the Cross Act after the reforming Tory home secretary who introduced it. This gave urban councils the power to clear 'unhealthy areas' by buying the houses compulsorily, evicting the tenants, demolishing the buildings and clearing the site. But when the site was empty the local authority could not build dwellings — although it could lay out sewers and streets for those who would. The site then had to be sold on to the association, which undertook to build dwellings for the number of people (but not the same people) who had been evicted in the first place.

In this way, housing associations were made the executors of state policy. In London, they built nearly 10,000 flats on Cross Act slum clearance sites, virtually all between 1878 and 1890. In London as a whole, between the 1840s and 1905, associations built a further 30,000 dwellings. This total of 40,000 can be compared with the combined efforts of all London local authorities before 1914, who built just 13,000 homes.

Until 1919 then, housing associations were in the front line of state-inspired housing provision and widely seen as the major providers outside private speculative development. But the inadequacy of this provision was starkly apparent — much less than 1,000 dwellings a year in the whole of London, for instance. And it was inadequate in one other respect too. For it became increasingly apparent that, despite early intentions, it was not 'the poor' who were benefiting from housing associations at all.

Providing improved housing was an explicit form of social imperialism for the early housing association reformers. Octavia

Hill probably represented most consciously their reforming
zeal. For her the urban working class was to be colonised in the
same way as Aborigines or Zulus in a different context. 'Truly
a wild, lawless, desolate little kingdom to come to rule over',
she wrote of an early experiment in buying a slum court in west
London and improving the houses. 'On what principles was I
to rule these people?' the queen of Marylebone asked herself:
'Firstly, to demand a strict fulfilment of their duties to me —
one of the chief of which would be the punctual payment of
rent; and secondly, to endeavour to be so unfailingly just and
patient, that they should learn to trust the rule that was over
them.'

Hill's system of intrepid visiting by lady rent collectors, with
the bailiffs as their stormtroopers, was applied not only in her
own schemes but by other associations also. In the 1880s, Miss
Cons kept the tenants of Surrey Buildings in check 'with that
peculiar mixture of sympathy and authority which characterises
the modern class of governing women.'

But this sort of controlling influence, exhausting no doubt for
all involved, could not be sustained for long. More and more
housing associations took the easy way out. Instead of reforming
difficult tenants, especially those too difficult to pay their rent,
they would get rid of them. Beatrice Webb, a rent collector on
the Hill system for a time in Wapping, put it succinctly in her
diary entry for 4 June 1885: 'Working hard. Buildings
unsatisfactory. Caretaker hopelessly inadequate. Tenants,
rough lot — the Aborigines of the east end. Pressure to exclude
these and take in only the respectable — follow Peabody's
example. Interview with the superintendent of Peabody's. "We
had a rough lot to begin with, had to weed them of the old
inhabitants — now only take in men with regular employment".'

Thus the poorest were excluded from the shelter envisaged
in Peabody's gift to 'the poor'. Housing associations relying on
making a dividend for their investors had even more reason to
follow suit. When the Four Per Cent Industrial Dwellings
Company developed a Spitalfields site in 1886-87, letting most
of the new flats to Jewish immigrants, they turned the class
make-up of the area on its head. The old slum houses had as
tenants street sellers, rag and bone dealers, labourers, dockers
— 70 per cent unskilled labour; the new flats were occupied

by tailors, cigarette makers, cabinet makers, even a few policemen — 70 per cent skilled. The urban poor would have to wait another 50 years for an interventionist state to begin to rehouse them in council housing as part of the slum clearance drives of the 1930s.

This is a fascinating moment to review the origins of the housing association movement in Britain. We live again in a time when charity is posited as the approved alternative to state intervention — when the plight of the homeless, the sick, the elderly and the young is exposed to us with open wounds in order that we should give where the state will not.

Private investment in working class housing is again courted by housing associations, who hawk their assets round City brokers and seek advice about privately-placed share issues — much as investors were wooed by Waterlow and others in the 1860s. Housing associations are once more explicitly the primary executors of a state housing policy which is at war with local authority provision, coming full circle to the Cross Act, and trying to demolish 60 years of state intervention on the way.

And again, the plight of the poorest, the most difficult, the least reliable, goes to the bottom of the pile as local authorities find themselves unable to cope even with the residual welfare housing role they now have.

A critical reviewer of Victorian philanthropy, writing in 1935, considered that the 19th century housing association movement, despite its provision for individual families, had signally failed to do the job it had set itself and which the state had set for it. In some ways, she thought, it had done more harm than good by obscuring the magnitude of the real problem with a false sense of achievement. Perhaps that, too, will be history's judgement on housing associations and the role given them by the Thatcher governments of the 1980s.

(This article was first published in ROOF, November 1989).

Chapter 2

Victorian values

A century ago, Charles Booth undertook the first major social survey of London. His work painted a unique picture of a world without adequate welfare systems and made the link between housing conditions and poverty.

Paul Spicker

It is over a hundred years since the first volume appeared of Charles Booth's *Life and labour of the people in London*. It was the beginning of a series of 17 volumes finally completed in 1903. The study began with a close examination of poverty in London; it developed with detailed examinations of every type of occupation, religious influence and municipal effort.

It was probably the first major social survey of the way that people lived, undertaken with a daunting comprehensiveness. Although Booth presented his work as a kind of census, it was much more; it involved a range of methods which were used to bring the study to life.

He described his work as a sort of 'photography' — a striking metaphor for 1889. The observations are at times stark, sentimental, provocative, and moralistic — Booth was very much a man of his time. The work had a major impact, for it provided the basis of the arguments for the introduction of old age pensions, and directly influenced the subsequent analysis of poverty.

Booth began by obtaining reports from School Board visitors about the condition of poor families. Initially, he and his investigators avoided going into the houses themselves, considering that it would be an 'unwarrantable impertinence' to 'meddle' with people's lives, but as the survey progressed, he wrote: 'We gained confidence, and made it a rule to see each street ourselves at the time we received the visitors' account of it.'

The picture that eventually emerged was a thorough analysis of London, street by street, with an assessment of the poverty and social class of the inhabitants.

The types of housing were graded mainly according to the degree of poverty of the people who lived in them, rather than the quality of the housing itself. The areas were graded by colour, so that their distribution could be plotted on a map.

The worst areas were coloured black on the maps. They were overcrowded and insanitary. 'In little rooms no more than eight feet square, would be found living father, mother and several children . . . Not a room would be free from vermin, and in many life at night was unbearable . . . Most of the doors stood open at night as well as all day, and the passage and the stairs gave shelter to many who were altogether homeless.'

The notes on households in black streets were given in the greatest detail. One example, somewhat abridged, will have to suffice: 'The story of the first floor in this house is one of the utmost horror. A man whose name I will not even pretend to give, by trade a sweep, having three grown-up sons, lived with and abused a woman to her death. She was an orphan brought up in an industrial school and had lived with him at least 11 years, having one child by him. She was good to the other children, as well as to her own child, and kind to the man. Wife and mother in every sense, except legally. But he so knocked her about that she was never free from bruises.

'The man had regular pay — 25s a week — and would spend nearly all in drink. He would swear at her, and kicks and blows would follow . . . She was got into a refuge, but he coaxed her back with fair words, with what results? . . . A few weeks later the poor woman lay on her bed unconscious, with blackened eye and face all bruised. She was dying . . . There was no prosecution, the neighbours shielded the man, and he too is now dead.'

The next class of houses were dark blue with black lines; the houses bore 'the look of great poverty'. For example: 'No. 7 Rydal Street: upper. Three rooms, four persons. Man, wife and two children. Labourer (nominal). A family of professional beggars. Always moving to escape rent. Lazy and filthy.'

Or: 'No. 6 Cleveland Terraces. Four rooms, seven persons. Man, wife and five children. Was in gasworks. Met with an accident and now cannot work. Clean respectable people. Great poverty.'

Dark blue houses had a poor environment, with large houses often subdivided into many smaller units. Of one street, Booth commented: 'The people who dwell here look as poverty-stricken as the houses'. People such as the residents of 'No.1 Latin Place South. Cottage. Rooms two, Persons eight. Man, wife and six young children. Gardener, out of work. Wife lately confined. Semi-starvation. Is helped by charity.

'No. 2 Latin Place South. Cottage. Rooms two, Persons five. Man, wife and three young children. Paralysed. Wife does mangling. Dreadful poverty.'

The better grades of property where poor people lived were light blue, purple and pink. A light blue street could still be judged 'rough and untidy', the houses 'ill cared for and shabby', like: 'No. 4 Little Merton Street. Two rooms, four people. Man, wife and two daughters. Cab-washer. A drunkard. Beats his wife and was in prison for it. Wife out late. Daughter wild.'

Purple streets contained a mixture of poverty and adequate housing. 'No. 38 Gordon Road. Six rooms, two persons. Old man and wife. Tailor, but crippled and paralysed. The wife was a school mistress. Are fairly well to do. Take a lodger sometimes.'

'No. 6 Turner Road. One room, four persons. Man, wife and two children. Was working at saw mills, but has been out of work for two months. Unthrifty wife. Dirty people.'

Pink streets were adequate, but they were not without their problems. Many old people, and families where there was unemployment, disability or widows, still appeared as poor. 'No. 43 Martin Street. Three rooms, four persons. Man, wife and two children. Blind. Has pension. Wife washes but is getting too old for it. Just manage. Poor.

'No. 23 Chesterfield Street is occupied in two rooms by a seaman and sailmaker, with wife and three children. He works at his trade half the year, and goes to sea the other half. Is sometimes badly off. Two of the children go to school, and the other is partially paralysed.'

The conclusions from the study were clear. Poverty was much more prevalent than it had been believed to be — nearly a third of the population of London was poor — and, although Booth was ready to blame many poor people for their poverty, there was also much poverty that arose without fault.

For Booth, housing conditions and poverty were closely linked. He defined poverty as a condition in which people had resources which were barely sufficient 'for a decent independent life'. Housing conditions were the clearest indication of people's material resources, because it showed what they were able to afford. Labourers, whose income seemed to be sufficient to have adequate housing, for example, lived in worse conditions than might be expected because their incomes were not secure, and they could not afford a more expensive commitment.

Booth put a great deal of emphasis on the importance of overcrowding as an indicator of poverty; as the research went on, he began to dismiss other evidence that people were poor if they were not overcrowded, although there were major problems evident in the early part of the survey through the incidence of sickness, disability and old age.

The maps revealed a distinct pattern of poverty in particular areas. It was clear to Booth that poor people lived, not just in bad housing conditions, but in poor areas. He refers, for example, to one area as 'a district where poverty is almost solid.' Some part of this was attributable to the social reputation of the area: 'A row of houses falls into bad repute, due merely to a few undesirable tenants who, if they are not ejected, render the neighbourhood too hot for anyone with a taste for decency.'

The judgement suggests that the tenants were 'bringing down' the area. But Booth did not, despite the received opinion of his time, and his own substantial prejudices, blame bad areas exclusively on the habits of the poor. Rather, he saw it as a combination of factors. One explanation which he favoured for the concentration of poverty was simple: people with adequate incomes were able to move out and improve their circumstances, and poor people were not.

But there are many other comments contained in *Life and labour*, particularly in the later volumes, about different influences on the spatial pattern of particular areas. For example, he notes at one point the effect of the layout and design of estates: 'In Battersea poverty is caught and held in successive railway loops south of the Battersea Park Road. . . . This is one of the best object-lessons in "poverty-traps" in London.'

It would be going too far to suggest that Booth had a clearly worked out model of the city, or of the processes through which such problems emerged. Booth's skill was as an observer; he recorded what he saw, believing that 'the facts' would speak for themselves. The importance of his study was that it revealed so much about the conditions people lived in.

The comprehensive approach of the survey meant that there was a great deal within it about the specific problems of housing, though this was not the central focus. Booth's work was unusual, for example, in trying to make an adequate assessment of the circumstances of single homeless people. He began with a study of common lodging houses — hostels, as we would now call them — though he argued that homelessness in such cases was an issue of lifestyle: 'From the luxury of the west end residential club to the "fourpenny doss" of Bangor Street or Short's Gardens is but a matter of degree.'

In Booth's day, there were over 30,000 people in this type of accommodation in central London; although there was a wide range of incomes, it disproportionately housed the poorest. Homeless people tended to move between lodging houses and sleeping rough. Unable to take a complete census, he took two samples from night shelters, including details of their age, employment, marital status and ethnic origin. Booth put special emphasis on a count taken after a long frost, when few people would be sleeping rough, but he was dissatisfied with the quality of the information, and he regretted that he could not supply more.

The main area in which the survey directly considers housing is in a discussion of blocks of flats, which were graded in relation to light, air and sanitation. Of one building, a four storey block graded 'very bad', there is the following comment: 'Everything is filthy, and the stench very bad. A few more steps lead to a dark passage with two-roomed or four one-roomed tenements. The floors above are similar. A notice outside tells passers that there are "rooms to let, painted and papered, and in good repair" and that "none but quiet respectable people need apply".'

Much of the material on blocks of flats was contributed by Octavia Hill, who wrote a section about their 'influence on character'. Hill tended to dismiss the importance of facilities and sanitation in favour of improving people's characters; to some extent, this runs counter to the survey's strong emphasis on poor physical conditions. However, her criticisms of flats as an environment for families were picked up by Booth in the final volume, and many of the reservations about this form of living still ring true.

When, at the end of the survey, Booth reviewed his material, he felt able to make some more general statements about bad housing. He described 12 classes of bad housing. They included old housing in bad condition, new housing that was badly built, housing with insufficient space, 'houses occupied by families of a class for which they are not designed and are not suited', insanitary houses, badly managed blocks, housing with excessive rents, and crowded homes.

Booth showed that he was aware, in a way that later commentators were not, that bad housing was not a simple issue. It was, rather, a combination of condition, design, management, social factors, and the use of the property. His analysis might have provided the basis for a reconsideration of housing policy for poor people. Sadly, unlike the material on poverty, it was to have virtually no discernible influence at all. Much of the current debate on poor council estates is going over the same ground — to the point where Booth's analysis seems relatively sophisticated.

It is difficult to say whether there is much to learn now from Booth's work. No-one would want to take on what he said uncritically, and many of the important points he made have been made again since. However, there are a number of valuable insights. Some are historical. Booth's survey reminds us of the vices of an unregulated private market — why public housing was necessary, and why private renting started to die off.

There are object lessons in the experience of life without an adequate system of social security benefits or health services. The study shows, too, that the link between poverty and poor areas is long standing, and that it applied in a very different housing market from that which we have now. Local authorities have been blamed for creating 'ghettos' but the ghettos existed long before the local authorities started to build.

There are, besides, a number of observations in the study about poverty which seem, in retrospect, well-founded. First, poverty, for many people, is all-embracing; problems of one type are strongly associated with problems of other types. Second, although poverty tends to be concentrated in poor areas, it is not confined to them; it is found in many places. Third, poor areas develop for a variety of reasons, including the pattern of industry, the type of housing, the reputation of an area, and the power of the residents to choose.

The power the study has stems not from its judgements or arguments, but the weight of material it accumulated. The evidence in Booth's study reinforces, and in many ways anticipates, an understanding of poverty which has taken a century to develop.

(This article was first published in ROOF, September 1989).

Chapter 3

A woman of her time

The work of 19th century housing reformer Octavia
Hill has attracted unstinting praise and aggressive
condemnation in almost equal measure.

David Clapham

Although Octavia Hill was not the originator of housing
management, she brought it to the forefront of debate on social
reform. Her recognition of the importance of the need for
trained housing workers laid the groundwork for the creation
of the housing management profession.

As an activity, housing management existed long before
Octavia Hill started her housing work in Paradise Place,
Marylebone, in 1865. However, it was mainly carried out by
professionals such as house agents, auctioneers and surveyors,
who all vied for pre-eminence. For many, housing management
was simply another source of income to supplement their main
activity.

Hill has continued to enjoy substantial prominence since her
death (the headquarters of the Institute of Housing is called
Octavia House). But she is a controversial figure who has, in
recent years, attracted both unstinting praise and aggressive
condemnation by writers attempting to show the relevance or
otherwise of her work to current problems. Hill was very much
a woman of her time, and to advocate the use of her methods
today is to misunderstand the context within which her work

took place. However much a return to Victorian values may be desired by some, the social context of housing work today is very different from the one she faced.

In the early 19th century, the pressures of industrial development, rapid population growth and the consequent poor living conditions in cities enlivened charitable enterprise at a time when state involvement in social affairs was almost non-existent, in accordance with the prevailing liberal attitude of *laissez-faire*. Philanthropy was also encouraged by a rise in evangelical Christianity which combined a strong emphasis on personal sacrifice and good works with an obsession with individual depravity. It also established a belief in the family as the paramount social institution and a desire to bring Christianity into the home. Thomas Chalmers, an influential Scottish religious reformer of the time, argued that the aim was to restore the social values of the countryside to large urban communities by giving the poor the kind of neighbourly supervision and assistance that would develop in them the qualities of self reliance and independence.

Thus, most parishes had their sewing classes and mothers' meetings, as well as 'visiting societies' to reach the homes of the poor. The focus on the family and the home meant that women were thought to be particularly well suited to charitable service. At a time when their opportunities were very limited, women's recognised high status in the home and family meant that they were at the forefront of religiously inspired attempts to extend family values to the community beyond the home. 'From their domestic citadel, they [women] made ever wider forays into society as the front-line defenders of family life'.[1]

State involvement in welfare in the mid-19th century was largely through relief provided under the Poor Law Amendment Act of 1834, and, in the case of the 'able-bodied' poor and their families, it meant the workhouse. As this was meant to be a last resort, conditions were spartan enough to deter all but the destitute. The poor were generally categorised into the 'deserving' and the 'undeserving'. Charitable effort was concentrated on the 'deserving', those who conformed to the moral values of the day and were prepared to exercise 'self-help' to deal with their problems, whilst the 'undeserving' were consigned to the care of the poor law. Philanthropists set out to avoid, at all costs, pauperising the poor — creating a dependence on handouts. 'Indiscriminate' relief was frowned upon and the emphasis was on visiting the poor in their own homes to spread christian values through individual contact and to provide practical help and advice on running the home and habits of cleanliness. 'In Britain they [philanthropists] sought to reform the family through a moral and physical cleaning of the nation's homes'.[2]

Octavia Hill was born in Wisbech in 1838. Her father, James Hill, was a merchant who was associated with many radical liberal causes of the time and endorsed the co-operative ideas of Robert Owen. Her mother, Caroline Hill, was the daughter of Dr Southwood Smith, a leading sanitary reformer, and contributed some radical writings on education. From an early age, Octavia was surrounded by talk of social reform and came into contact with many of the leading social reformers of the day.

When Octavia was in her early teens, her father suffered a breakdown in health brought on by the collapse in his business. Caroline Hill and her family were left with no income and with business debts to repay. Caroline took Octavia and some of her sisters to London where they were forced to earn their living. Unlike most Victorian philanthropists, Octavia was dogged by personal financial insecurity until the later stages of her life. In London, Octavia worked as the supervisor of a toy-making workroom for poor children and experienced at first hand their atrocious living conditions. It was also during this early period in London that Octavia's religious convictions grew. She was much influenced by the teaching of F D Maurice who, like many other reformers of the time, placed emphasis on helping the poor through personal contact and decried any form of 'indiscriminate' charity, which he claimed would breed dependency.

These ideas were accepted by Octavia Hill and rigidly adhered to in all her subsequent work. She wrote in 1869: 'There are two main principles to be observed in any plan for raising the poorest class in England. One is that personal influence must be brought strongly to bear on the individuals. The other is that the rich must abstain from any form of alms giving.'[3]

Octavia's ideas then were not original, but reflected contemporary thinking about social reform. Her contribution was not in the philosophy of reform, but rather in its application through her work with poor people.

Octavia Hill's disquiet at the habits of the poor, gained from her experiences with the children in her workroom and their families, was matched by a disapproval of the behaviour of many landlords. She criticised them for not keeping their properties in good repair, for permitting overcrowding through sub-letting and for allowing arrears of rent to accrue. She longed to show that if a landlord's duties were carried out in a businesslike way, it would be possible to provide reasonable conditions and yet still make a reasonable return on investment. Housing reform could thus be achieved without charity or public subsidy from the tax- or rate-payer.

At the same time she saw management of houses as a means of making personal contact with the poor to 'urge them to rouse themselves from the lethargy and indolent habits into which they have fallen'.[4]

Hill got the chance to implement her ideas when a friend, John Ruskin, was persuaded to buy some properties in Marylebone and install her as manager. The properties (and most of her subsequent ones) were in a very poor state of repair when she took them over. Sanitary facilities were inadequate and often dilapidated. Windows were broken and covered with rags and paper. Rooms were overcrowded, sometimes damp and had plaster falling from the walls and fire-grates collapsing into the room. Overcrowding was rife and large arrears of rent were common. The tenants were the poorest who could afford their own room. Hill never attempted to house the very poorest, who were without a settled abode. When rooms became vacant they were improved, and tenants who showed signs of responding well to her requirements were offered them.

Other improvements were only carried out when tenants were deemed to deserve them and they could be paid for out of a surplus from rents. Overcrowded families were encouraged to take on extra rooms when they became available, and sub-letting was forbidden. Eviction was threatened if arrears of rent were incurred, or if tenants did not otherwise meet Hill's standards. Tenants of low moral standards — the 'undeserving' poor — were summarily evicted, and she records one case where a man was threatened with eviction if he did not send his children to school.

The key to Octavia Hill's 'system' was the personal relationship between the landlord and tenant. She tried to re-create in urban areas the traditional paternalism of the country landowner with his tenants. Her visits to collect rent were seen as opportunities to develop personal respect and friendship, to offer support and advice, and occasionally offer material help where this would not pauperise the recipient. She employed some of the older girls to scrub the stairs in order to give them experience of work and to foster a sense of pride in the property. She also employed some of her male tenants to carry out repairs to the property, holding back jobs to help tide them over periods of unemployment.

Hill adopted many contemporary philanthropic activities. She tried to find some communal space in her blocks which could be used for sewing classes, mothers' meetings and other charitable work. She tried to provide areas for children to play (under the watchful eye of a supervisor to organise their games) and to provide some greenery to brighten up her tenants' lives.

Hill was successful in improving the conditions of the properties in her care whilst making a five per cent return for the owner. She also claimed to have helped many of her tenants 'improve' themselves, although it would be interesting to know what her tenants felt about her efforts. As news of her work spread, she was offered more properties by bodies such as the Ecclesiastical Commissioners. She recruited volunteers to manage the properties for her and trained them in bookkeeping, sanitary science and landlord and tenant law as well as in the practical skills of dealing with tenants. They were also required to be familiar with the activities of other agencies working for the poor.

Hill was adamant that the key to her work was a set of principles, not a detailed system. Therefore, she operated in a very decentralised way, with her workers being given their own properties to manage and the flexibility to meet the principles in their own ways.

The principles which underpinned Octavia Hill's management method also determined her increasingly sought-after views on contemporary issues. She was influential in the drafting of the Artisans' and Labourers' Dwellings Improvement Act, 1875 (the Cross Act) which gave local authorities the powers to purchase and demolish 'unhealthy' areas of unfit housing. She also gave evidence to the Royal Commission on the Housing of the Working Classes in 1884.

Hill's views on housing reform were built on her principle that the management of houses should go hand in hand with social work with the tenants. 'You cannot deal with the people and their homes separately . . . the people's homes are bad, partly because their habits and lives are what they are. Transplant them tomorrow to a healthy and commodious home and they would pollute and destroy them.'

For this reason she was highly critical of the activities of many of the model dwelling companies (the other major form of philanthropic housing activity) for not placing enough emphasis on personal contact with tenants. Also, she criticised their preoccupation with the building of new blocks of flats with good sanitary facilities, quite rightly arguing that this form of provision was out of the reach of the poorest and worst housed families. Therefore, she was in favour of the improvement of existing properties to minimal standards in order that a poorer class of tenant could be helped. She also criticised the model dwelling companies for the building of large blocks of flats, which she considered detrimental to family life, rather than cottages.

Hill reserved most criticism for the idea that councils should build and manage housing. Like most contemporary philanthropists, she had a profound distrust of the state. She felt that public subsidy for housing was indiscriminate help which would pauperise the poor. She also disliked the idea of tenants being able to vote for their landlord through local elections — an arrangement which she held was open to abuse.

Towards the end of the 19th century, Octavia Hill began to look increasingly out of step with the times. Her dislike of state involvement placed her in a policy backwater as the state moved inexorably into deeper involvement in housing issues. Also, the social and economic conditions of the time meant that she felt herself unable to guarantee a return of five per cent to owners of property, and so her approach began to seem less viable.

Ruskin Gallery

Octavia Hill, social reformer, philanthropist and early housing manager.

Octavia Hill was undoubtedly a woman of strong personal qualities which qualify her to stand alongside the other great women philanthropists of the age. Her work was not confined to housing; her love of the countryside led her to become one of the founder members of the National Trust.

Her passion for social reform also led her to take an active and leading role in the Charity Organisation Society which, through its personal visiting of the poor, was the forerunner of modern social work practice. This work led to her being appointed to the Royal Commission on the Poor Law which sat between 1905 and 1909.

It is difficult to assess Hill's contribution to housing. She offered little new thinking on social reform as she was heavily influenced by the contemporary ideas of others, but her original contribution was to link concern for reforming the poor with the management of housing. Her ideas on housing policy were sought after and respected, but were increasingly ignored. It is interesting to speculate, however, whether subsidies for house building, often discussed in the early years of the 20th century, might have been introduced before 1919 had Octavia Hill supported rather than vehemently opposed them.

Through her practical work she was able to improve the housing conditions of a significant number of people, although it is impossible to estimate how many, because with her devolved system of responsibility she was unable to work out the number of properties managed under her method. Whatever the number, however, it was clearly very small in relation to the total number of households. Her influence on model dwelling companies and on private landlords and managing agents was minimal. Her prominence was out of all proportion to the size of the practical contribution she made.

Octavia Hill's management method has exerted a continuing if limited influence over housing management practice. With the growth of council housing after the First World War, the management task was usually split between a number of existing local authority departments and was seen as an administrative activity rather than as a means of reforming the poor. Hill's ideas were kept alive by the Society of Women Housing Estate Managers (later to merge with the Institute of Housing) formed by her supporters and with a membership largely confined to the voluntary sector. Some local authorities adopted the Octavia Hill system and appointed women 'visitors', but they were in a small minority. However, although the ideas were not widely implemented by local authorities, they survived and resurfaced at times of concern about housing management. For example, the Central Housing Advisory Committee, in its investigation of housing management in 1935, received evidence from Octavia Hill's supporters, and gave guarded support for their work.

Four factors have led to a renewed interest in Octavia Hill's ideas in recent years: the predominant concern with the management of existing stock rather than with development issues; the increasing concentration of poor people in the public rented sector; the emergence of hard-to-let estates; and the acceptance in some political quarters of the need for a return to Victorian values.

Advocates of Octavia Hill's approach, such as Anne Power, claim that the basic problems facing housing management today are 'strikingly similar in many details to the housing conditions of the late 19th century.'[5]

However, even strong advocates express reservations about Hill's firm christian beliefs and her authoritarianism based on a particular set of moral values. Octavia Hill was adamant that what were worth following were the basic principles which her management system was designed to achieve, rather than the system itself, which she recognised would have to be flexible to meet changing circumstances. Undaunted, present day advocates promote her management method, but reject the principles underlying it.

Others reject both Octavia Hill's principles and her method, and blame her influence for most of the perceived problems of housing management. For example, Spicker blames her for the continuing over-use of eviction as a management tool; the over-emphasis on cleanliness; and for widespread grading of poor tenants into deserving and undeserving. He argues that Octavia Hill's moralistic and authoritarian approach is inconsistent with, and undermines, current ideas of basic rights to welfare, which he argues underpin the modern welfare state.[6]

Advocates and opponents make the mistake of over-emphasising Octavia Hill's personal contribution. She evidently had remarkable personal qualities. But her work was based on social principles which were widely held at the time. Support for, or criticism of, Octavia Hill's approach tends to imply comment on Victorian society itself or to be based on the misguided belief that her management method, and the principles on which it is based, can be uprooted from their context and transported forward to a completely different set of political, social, economic and institutional circumstances.

The true value of a study of Octavia Hill's principles and methods is not in their current applicability but in those questions raised about housing management which are relevant to the current situation. Some aspects of her work seem to coincide with current ideas of good practice, noticeably her localised and devolved approach. Others are less in tune with current practice.

For example, the close association between social work and housing management raises questions about the current role of the latter, with the concentration of disadvantaged people in the public rented sector and the government's stated commitment to community care. Should housing management adopt a more welfare-orientated role than at present, or at least improve its links with social work?

Hill's authoritarianism and her intention to use housing management to control and change the behaviour of tenants leads to interesting questions about the accountability of housing management today. Is it accountable to tenants, housing professionals, political representatives, or a wider social interest? To what extent should housing management be accountable to tenants? Finally, Octavia Hill sometimes employed her own tenants to carry out work on her properties in order to help them over difficult times. In the current context, this raises questions about the integration of housing and economic development. To what extent, and how, can housing be used to generate employment?

These are important questions which a study of Octavia Hill's work raises but, despite the vogue for all things Victorian, cannot be expected to answer. Remarkable though she was, she could never have even envisaged many of the issues and problems in housing today.

Notes

1. F Prochaska, *The voluntary impulse — philanthropy in modern Britain*, Faber and Faber, 1988.
2. *Ibid.*
3. G Darley, *Octavia Hill — a life*, Constable, 1990.
4. O Hill, *Homes of the London poor*, Macmillan, 1875.
5. A Power, *Property before people — the management of twentieth-century council housing*, Allen and Unwin, 1987.
6. P Spicker, 'Legacy of Octavia Hill', Housing magazine, June 1985.

(This article was first published in ROOF, January 1991).

Chapter 4

Improving poor housing

Unlike other areas of public health policy, legal standards on housing are basic, and still reflect a period when houses were little more than unserviced shells.

Pat Garside

The significance of poor housing for ill-health has been recognised by public health reformers since the early 19th century. Edwin Chadwick, the guiding hand of the Victorian sanitary movement, argued that overcrowded houses ranked alongside industrial waste, polluted rivers, slaughterhouses and filth as one of the major threats to the 'health, personal safety or the conveniences of the subject'. Yet in significant respects, government intervention in raising housing standards has been reluctant, spasmodic and weak compared with other areas of public health.

This is particularly true for existing houses. In the case of new housing — whether on greenfield or clearance sites — the record is much better. Government has been active here since 1858, when local authorities first gained the power to make by-laws to control new buildings and streets without having to secure a private local act. Successive reports of the Tudor Walters Committee (1918), the Dudley Committee (1944) and the Parker Morris Committee (1961) set standards for council housing far in advance of prevailing designs not only in the public but also in the private sector. Furthermore, building regulations have established specific and relatively stringent controls over the technical standards of new dwellings.

Yet the overall impact of these standards was bound to be limited, since at best new building adds a mere two per cent a year to the existing stock. Even after the building boom of the interwar years, only a third of the housing stock was new in 1939. Today, a third of existing houses constructed before 1919, and many of the rapidly built interwar estates, are themselves showing the 'tooth of time', as they approach the end of their 60 year life. In addition, the problems of much postwar local authority stock are causing concern.

It is the setting of standards to identify and manage such problems of housing obsolescence that has raised, and continues to raise, fundamental problems for government.

From 1919 until the late 1960s, housing policy and local government activity mainly focused on the development of new estates and (intermittently) on slum clearance. For those who benefited directly, the change in housing standards was dramatic. Yet for most people, raising the standard of existing houses would have been a much more far-reaching way of improving housing conditions. Here though, the law remained silent until 1957, when an 'unfitness standard' was finally embodied in housing law.

Even this represented something of a pyrrhic victory for housing reformers since the legal standard adopted by the 1957 Housing Act was based, virtually word for word, on a Ministry of Health *Manual on unhealthy areas* published in 1919. The standard was brief, basic and woefully out of date. Even in 1919, the Ministry's *Manual* had acknowledged that it represented not the desirable, but the very minimum standard. Yet this set the limits for government intervention from 1957 until 1989, when the Local Government and Housing Act introduced a new standard.

This latest standard, which came into effect in April 1990, is an advance on the one it replaces, but nevertheless still lags many decades behind people's expectations. It finally acknowledges the importance of the provision of artificial lighting and heating for housing fitness, as well as the need for amenities such as a bath and toilet. Yet local authorities have been advised that the measure of 'adequacy' for the purpose of the Act is danger to the health and safety of occupants, rather than their comfort.

In practice this means that adequacy continues to be measured at a very basic level even in areas such as heating where there is clear evidence of health risks if temperatures fail to reach the 'comfort' level of 18c in main living rooms, and 16c elsewhere. The new standard is not sufficiently concerned with energy efficiency and thermal performance of dwellings and fails to ensure that occupants can maintain the levels of warmth required without excessive cost. The clear evidence of the central importance of warmth and lack of dampness in houses for health is not recognised, despite the changes.

Two questions emerge from these reflections on the history of housing standards. Why has government been so reluctant to intervene? What protection have housing standards provided for those continuing to live in the worst housing, both in the past and in the present day?

In human affairs, the word 'standard' is capable of widely different interpretations. Standards may be used to determine minimal levels of performance, or they may be a rallying call to excellence. While we may see standards for new houses as fitting the latter interpretation, standards for older houses have definitely fallen within the former.

Legislators have been less cautious in other areas affecting public health. Consider the contrast, for example, with the motor car. No-one would consider that rules designed for cars in 1919 should still be applied 80 years later. Yet house design changed at least as much as car design from the days when only two per cent of houses were wired for electricity and a quarter of London's households kept servants.

In 1919, 90 per cent of recently-built houses in Birmingham had no internal toilet and none at all had a bathroom. Moreover, a third of the population lived in houses built in the 19th century.

Compared with the highly detailed and dauntingly precise MoT test, however, housing standards have reflected a period when houses were unserviced shells, with walls, doors and windows but precious little else. Even the latest housing standard has no equivalent of the MoT's specific testing of particular components to precise standards — no test for dampness, thermal performance, water supply or drainage equivalent to the tests for car brakes, tyres and indicator lights.

Yet the threat to people's health from their homes is greater than the threat from the roads, even if we only look at fatalities and accidents. In the 1980s, 6,000 people a year were killed on the roads, and 334,000 were injured. In the same period, accidental deaths in the home numbered around 4,500 annually, while more than two million people needed hospital treatment following home accidents. Since people's health can also suffer from poor housing in many other less dramatic, but equally distressing, ways, why are the criteria for housing standards not as clear, measurable and incontrovertible as those for cars? Why are the penalties not similarly instantaneous, with no right of appeal?

Recently, the government has intervened even more fundamentally, by requiring the wearing of safety belts in cars. This is in direct contrast to its prevailing view of housing. Defending the view that a person's housing conditions are one's own affair, one minister told Parliament that if people wanted to spend their money on foreign holidays rather than on repairing their homes, then that was none of his concern! In this case, the government is willing to impose standards on drivers and their passengers even where there is no risk to any third party. Within the home, on the other hand, where there is bound to be a risk to other people from poor conditions, the government declares that standards are essentially a private matter outside the sphere of law.

The example of test standards for cars is not the only area of public health where housing sanctions lag behind. Where food is concerned, there are powers and regulations that give both officials and customers very much greater control than they have over housing. The principles underlying food control have much more in common with MoT tests than they have with housing standards. Firstly, there is no requirement that failures in food *must* be injurious to health before action can be taken. No bread manufacturer, for example, dare allow one fly to get into a single loaf for fear of prosecution, even though after baking, the 'foreign body' is, to all intents and purposes, harmless. Producers are open to prosecution under the Food and Drugs Acts for offering food for sale 'not of the nature, substance and quality demanded by the purchaser'.

Yet what landlord can be prosecuted for offering a flat to rent 'not of the nature, substance and quality' demanded by the tenant? What owner occupier offering property for sale faces such a requirement? Why must an infestation of fleas in a house have to be demonstrably a threat to health before redress can be sought? Why the difference from the case of a single, harmless dead fly? On this, as on many aspects of housing standards, the law is passive and the rule of *'caveat emptor'* (buyer beware) applies.

How has this situation arisen? First, partly through the sensitivity of English law — both common and statute law — to rights of property. Ownership of property confers more rights than ownership of cars. Housing is regarded as a different kind of good from other items of consumer spending. The Englishman's home is indeed a castle. While the earlier slum clearance schemes did represent a substantial interference with property rights, compulsory purchase orders were directed primarily against private landlords — a dwindling and, it seemed, undesirable class of owner — rather than against owner occupiers.

Depriving owner occupiers of their homes because they are unfit is intervention of a different order from slaughtering infected animals, or taking deficient cars off the road, not least because, in the case of the unfit house, action triggers duties and responsibilities on the part of local authorities that they do not always welcome, especially when their resources are meagre.

Second, the extent of poor conditions in existing housing has often been so great that neither local authorities nor central government have wanted to acknowledge the true extent of the problem. They have therefore been extremely careful to set standards at a level that made the situation appear manageable.

Furthermore, it is important to realise that legislators have set housing standards with very specific objectives in mind and not as a general means of identifying *all* unfit houses. The 1957 standard was set at a time when private building was booming, and local authorities were being directed for the first time since the 1930s towards slum clearance. Indeed, Exchequer subsidies

The standard as set down in the 1957 Housing Act Section 4 is as follows:-

'In determining for any purposes of this Act, whether a house is unfit for human habitation, regard shall be held to its condition in respect of the following matters, that is to say —

(a) repairs
(b) stability
(c) freedom from damp
(d) internal arrangement
(e) natural lighting
(f) ventilation
(g) water supply
(h) draining and sanitary conveniences
(i) facilities for preparation and cooking of food and for the disposal of waste water

and the house shall be deemed to be unfit as aforesaid if, and only if, it is so far defective in one or more of said matters that it is not reasonably suitable for occupation in that condition'.

for building by local authorities were being withdrawn except in association with clearance. The 1957 definition was therefore devised to mark the boundary within which local authorities could take compulsory action leading to dispossession and clearance.

The revised standard of fitness set down in the 1989 Local Government and Housing Act has been established in a completely different context. Clearance activity is currently at its lowest level since before the First World War. The aim now is to use the standard to ration public resources available to people for improving their homes. The new standard is part of a filtering process intended to target public resources onto the poorest people, living in the worst properties, with the emphasis on improvement, rather than clearance and rebuilding. The unfitness standard has become an instrument of welfare provision, rather than of housing policy.

Throughout this century, standards have been set to control the visibility of the problem. Limited visions required limited solutions. Even Chadwick, who acknowledged the wretchedness of 'dark, damp, and incommodious habitations,'

The revised standard set out in the Local Government and Housing Act 1989 is as follows:-

'604(1) A dwelling house is fit for human habitation for the purposes of this Act unless, in the opinion of the local housing authority, it fails to meet one or more of the requirements in paragraphs (a) to (i) below and, by reason of that failure, is not reasonably suitable for occupation, —

(a) it is structurally stable;

(b) it is free from serious disrepair;

(c) it is free from dampness prejudicial to health of the occupants (if any);

(d) it has adequate provision for lighting, heating and ventilation;

(e) it has adequate piped supply of wholesome water;

(f) there are satisfactory facilities in the dwelling-house for the preparation of and cooking of food, including a sink with a satisfactory supply of hot and cold water;

(g) it has suitably located water-closet for the exclusive use of the occupants (if any);

(h) it has, for the exclusive use of the occupants (if any), a suitably located fixed bath or shower and wash-hand basin each of which is provided with a satisfactory supply of hot and cold water; and

(i) it has an effective system for the draining of foul, waste and surface water

and any reference to a dwelling-house being unfit for human habitation shall be construed accordingly.

Whether or not a dwelling-house which is a flat satisfies the requirements in subsection (1), it is unfit for human habitation for the purposes of this Act if, in the opinion of the local housing authority, the building or a part of the building outside the flat fails to meet one or more of the requirements in paragraphs (a) to (e) below and, by reason of that failure, the flat is not reasonably suitable for occupation, —

(a) the building or part is structurally stable;

(b) it is free from serious disrepair;

(c) it is free from dampness;

(d) it has adequate provision for ventilation; and

(e) it has an effective system for the draining of foul, waste and surface water.'

nevertheless chose drainage as his priority, on the grounds that this was 'the primary and most important measure, and at the same time the most practicable and within the recognised province of public administration.'

Despite the rhetoric of reformers, legislators have been less concerned with raising the general level of conditions in the worst housing, and more with defining the limits of state responsibility. The business of setting housing standards has been an exercise in damage limitation, rather than a comprehensive policy for substandard housing.

Today the question of housing standards is entering a new phase. Most people in Britain today are well housed. In 1957, by contrast, probably the majority of people were very badly housed. Nowadays, serious problems are confined to groups who appear to command neither resources nor political influence. They suffer very poor housing conditions, and yet at the same time they find themselves excluded even from the rudimentary protection that the law affords. There are few signs that policy makers are prepared to recognise and remedy this situation.

Powers in relation to hostels and other multiple-occupied housing, for example, have recently been amplified and strengthened, but the level of local authority activity remains very low. New regulations came into force in July 1991 following substantial amendments to Part XI of the 1985 Housing Act. These can provide a basic framework for improving the management and physical standards of housing in multiple occupation (HMOs), but much depends on enforcement action by local authorities.

For example, there is now a standard of fitness covering means of escape from fire, the adequacy of amenities relative to the numbers of occupants, and the state of repair of the dwelling and common parts as a whole. But action remains discretionary on the part of local authorities, except in the minority of cases where the HMO has more than three storeys and 500 square metres or more of floor space.

Powers in relation to hotels used for housing homeless families are even more circumscribed. It has been judged unreasonable for local authorities to use their powers under the Housing Acts to improve facilities in bed and breakfast hotels once they have placed families there. Improvements can only be demanded before the use of particular premises for such accommodation. This is very difficult to achieve in practice, since homeless families are placed by housing departments of local authorities while enforcement of housing standards is the responsibility of environmental health departments.

Rising numbers of homeless households and a dwindling council stock has encouraged increasing use of caravans and mobile homes by local authorities. Yet standards applied to caravans and mobile homes often reflect their original use as holiday homes rather than their current use as year-round long term residences. Because such structures are not regarded as dwellings for the purposes of housing law, they are exempt from their protection. They cannot be subject to clearance orders except as part of a scheme consisting predominantly of ordinary houses. They cannot be condemned as unfit, and are not subject to overcrowding standards. Building controls do not apply. Remedies for intolerable conditions are only available through the statutory nuisance provisions of the Environmental Protection Act 1990, where it is necessary to prove that circumstances are 'prejudicial to the health of the occupants' or constitute a nuisance to the neighbours.

Significant numbers of deprived groups — people with low incomes, especially the elderly, young single people and single parents — find themselves, not totally excluded from mainstream housing, but confined to the very poorest sections of the public rented and owner occupied sectors. In these cases too, existing law designed to identify and remedy intolerable housing conditions does not apply.

This is not so much a deliberate omission as a reflection of the historical circumstances in which the legislation was framed. The major focus is assumed to be the private rented sector — still the dominant tenure in the 1950s. The Housing Acts cannot be enforced against local authority housing and here, too, tenants only have recourse to the Environmental Protection Act. Though the legislation can be applied to owner occupied houses, the severe procedural and practical difficulties of doing so mean that action is very rarely taken.

The future for those in bad housing today looks grim, given the difficulties experienced in the past in raising standards in existing houses through statutory means. In mainstream owner occupied housing, the matter will be left in the hands and the resources of private individuals, except where both owners *and* their property are so poor that they qualify for state grants.

Residual housing — private rented accommodation, especially that in multiple occupation, temporary dwellings and run-down council housing estates — will continue to suffer the very worst conditions, beyond the reach of even the very low housing standards embodied in law.

Given the relative powerlessness of the people in these forms of housing, the continuing decline in public spending on housing and the depression in the housing market, it is very difficult to envisage any swift or decisive action to remedy the situation.

(This article was first published in ROOF, March 1990, and updated in December 1991).

Chapter 5

Striking out on Red Clyde

Glasgow's celebrated rent strike gave rise to 70 years of rent control, and demonstrated the power of working class communities in Scotland to defeat unpopular measures.

Seán Damer

Popular culture in Scotland has long reflected a hatred of landlords and their agents, factors. In 1784, Robert Burns wrote in the *Twa Dugs*:

'I've noticed, on our Laird's *court-day*,
An' mony a time my heart's been wae,
Poor *tenant-bodies*, scant o' cash,
Hoe they maun thole a *factor's* snash★:
He'll stamp an' threaten, curse an' swear.
He'll apprehend them, *poind* their gear,
While thy maun stand, wi aspect humble
An' hear it a', and fear an' tremble!'
★*Snash is a Scots word meaning abuse.*

Such popular feeling towards property owners and their factors in the city of Glasgow stemmed from the fact that a substantial proportion of the city's population historically came from the Highlands of Scotland. They were dispossessed people, victims of the ruthless land clearances. They had every reason to bring bitter feelings towards landlords with them, and these are

expressed in many songs and poems, and in the oral culture of
the Gaels.

Similarly, an even larger section of Glasgow's population
came from Ireland, penniless victims of the 1840s famine and
the later land wars. The Irish too were bitter against the
landlords who had thrown them off the land, and again this was
expressed in song. Such a population, grossly overcrowded in
Glasgow's slum tenements, was a very volatile one.

The property-owners of Glasgow and their factors (agents)
were organised in powerful cartels which dominated the private
rented market, the biggest housing sector in Glasgow until the
Second World War. In the decades before the First World
War, they were utterly ruthless. The Scottish legal system was
on their side, and armed them with a galaxy of legislation which
they did not hesitate to use — warrant sales, arrestment of
wages, evictions.

Factors also issued a 'line' or reference to their tenants, and
this was a powerful weapon for controlling tenants who
complained about the disrepair of their houses, or who objected
to exorbitant rents. Lack of a line meant that no factor in the
city would grant a tenancy in a decent tenement house, and so
the unfortunate tenant would be driven to seek accommodation
in a slum.

It was the factors who bore the brunt of popular discontent
about this system as they were the people who dealt with the
public on a day-to-day basis. The antipathy felt towards them
by working class people can be gauged from the stories in the
annual Christmas pantomimes in Glasgow at the turn of the
century. In every single one, the factor, 'Mr Money Bags', is a
figure of derision.

In the first couple of decades of this century, the records of
the Sheriff Courts show a staggering annual list of applications
for warrants for 'ejectment' — eviction, arrestment of wages,
poinding and warrant-sales. 'Poinding' (pronounced 'pinding')
meant seizing and selling the goods of a debtor. The 'law of
urban hypothec' in Scotland said that a tenant's 'furniture,
furnishing, and tools are liable to sequestration by a landlord
immediately after they enter on possession of a house as security
for rent not then accrued, due, or payable.' Failure to pay the

rent, or failure to pay the full term of the rent in advance, gave
the landlord or his factor the right to act. And they did.

The tenants of Glasgow fought back in every way they could,
and rent and housing issues dominated Clydeside working class
politics from the start of this century. Local tenants had the
legal right to lodge an objection against a warrant or eviction,
and this they did in their thousands, actively encouraged by
John Wheatley, Mary Barbour and Andrew MacBride of the
Independent Labour Party-inspired Scottish Labour Housing
Association.

Women would pack the stair when a sheriff officer came to
carry out an eviction and make it impossible for him to move.
Sheriffs were often pelted with rubbish, or thrown into the
midden, the communal refuse heap in the backcourts of the
tenements. Similarly, if the sheriff officers came to execute a
warrant sale, to forcibly sell the tenant's goods in order to pay
arrears of rent, locals would pack the sale, buy their neighbour's
things for a pittance, and drive off dealers and outsiders with
threats of violence.

In the case of evictions, and particularly during the protracted
rent strike in Clydebank during the 1920s, neighbours would
put the evicted person's furniture back into the house and
re-occupy it. The ultimate weapon tenants had against grasping
factors was to do a 'moonie', a moonlight flit, and this was a
common occurrence.

Matters came to a head in the celebrated Glasgow Rent Strike
in 1915. With thousands of men away at the front, the city was
flooded with munitions workers from elsewhere in Britain. The
factors took the opportunity of this monopoly on scarce
accommodation to raise rents. There was immediate uproar.

The Glasgow Labour Housing Association called an
immediate rent strike, and soon whole streets in the city were
displaying placards in their windows: 'Rent Strikes Against
Increases: We Are Not Removing.' The Housing Association,
in conjunction with local women, organised street committees
to ensure that the strike was solid, and to resist any attempts at
eviction for non-payment of the increased rent. The housewives
were equipped with handbells to ring should a sheriff officer
be seen, and would physically pack the stair to prevent the
eviction being carried out.

But the factors' greed was such that they took some
rent-striking Govan shipyard workers to the Sheriff Court to
get their wages arrested to pay off the arrears of rent. This was
a move of monumental stupidity. The women of Govan went
down to the yards and brought the men out. The word went
round like wildfire. Thousands of demonstrators converged on
the Sheriff Court. A delegation of workers told the Sheriff that
if he convicted the rent strikers, there would be a general strike
on the Clyde the next day. Faced with such a possibility in
Britain's main munitions-producing area in the middle of a war
which was not going well, the government caved in.

A Rent Restriction Act was rushed through Parliament which
froze rents at the pre-war level. This was a major victory for the
working class movement. In spite of numerous efforts on the
part of property owners to remove it, the principle of rent
restrictions was firmly established, and was to remain in force
for the next half century. It was the beginning of the end of the
arbitrary power of factors and property owners in Glasgow.

These issues were a part of everyday experience in Glasgow
until the Second World War, fuelled the Red Clyde movement,
and informed all aspects of local working class culture. They
were also a central part of the experience of local women, for
it was they who had to manage the household budget, deal in
the affairs of the stair and street, resist eviction, threaten dealers
at warrant sales, and cope with the factor's snash. It would be
hard to underestimate the depth of feeling on Clydeside on
these issues.

And yet, in 1990, Strathclyde regional council did just that.
Marx once said that history repeats itself, the first time as
tragedy, the second time as farce. What went on in 1990 with
the poll tax verges on the farcical.

When the poll tax was introduced, the Labour party went
along with it, even to the extent of drawing up the legal
machinery for putting the detested poinding and warrant sales
into operation. This resulted in massive popular disgust.

By July 1990, a third of Glasgow's population had refused
to pay the poll tax — well over 200,000 people. In March,
Strathclyde regional council issued 145,000 summary warrants
in the city. The local anti-poll tax campaign was exceptionally
well organised, and distributed information sheets telling

tenants their rights and providing hot-line telephone numbers. They drew on the lessons of Glasgow's history, saying that the letters sheriff officers sent out informing tenants of an impending warrant sale were terrorising them into paying the poll tax.

In various 'at risk' neighbourhoods, there were mobile patrols with walkie-talkie radios to organise should a sheriff officer be spotted on his way to carry out a warrant sale. Modern technology replaced the handbells used by the women of Glasgow in 1915 for exactly the same purpose! In a manner strikingly reminiscent of the 1915 Rent Strike in the city, ordinary Glaswegians learnt that the only way to bring down the poll tax was to organise themselves in their neighbourhoods, keep in touch with other areas and be on the alert.

There is a photograph of a group of women in the area of Partick, where I live, blocking a stair during the 1915 Rent Strike. It says 'God Help the Sheriff Officer Who Tries to Enter Here.' The same held good in 1990.

(This article was first published in ROOF, July 1990).

Chapter 6

From mutual interests to market forces

From humble self-help organisations set up to house the better-off working class, building societies have grown into the complex financial institutions we know today.

Martin Boddy

The 1986 Building Societies Act, the first comprehensive overhaul of the legislative framework in over a hundred years, represented a watershed in building society history. The full implications of this radical rethink of their role in both the finance and housing markets are still being worked through in practice — and recession in the early 1990s slowed the pace of change. But it forms a suitable vantage point from which to look back over the history and development of the societies.

The first recorded society is reckoned to be that founded at the Golden Cross Inn, Birmingham, in 1775, soon followed by others in the Midlands and North. The very first building societies were mutual, self-help organisations set up to meet the housing needs of better-off working class migrants to the rapidly expanding industrial towns. The Longridge Building Society, set up near Preston in 1793, listed among its members weavers, yeomen, stonemasons, a carpenter and a cotton spinner.

Legal recognition of building societies as corporate bodies, distinct from banks or companies, came with the 1836 Building Societies Act. It was the 1874 Building Societies Act, however, following an 1872 Royal Commission, which provided what was to be the remarkably durable framework for societies' later expansion.

In the early days, a small group of members would meet regularly, usually at first in an inn. As regular investment, or 'subscriptions', built up, they allocated to each member in turn the value of a standard 'share' in the society. This was then, typically, £150, around the sum required to buy or purchase a house. Practices varied. Some of the early societies, rather than paying out funds as a lump sum, in effect acted as developer. They would, themselves, acquire land and organise the building of houses which were then allocated to members — hence 'building societies'.

The order in which members received their 'share' or house might be decided by drawing lots. In other cases, members bid for shares, paying a premium, a form of interest, on top of the nominal value which served to swell the society's funds. Members who received their share or house first obviously continued paying in on a regular basis. Subscriptions continued until all members had received a lump sum share or a house. The society then terminated.

These early 'terminating societies' soon started accepting money from investors, to speed up the rate at which funds available to members accumulated. Loans were repaid, with interest, out of members' subscriptions. It was from this that the modern 'permanent' building society, with separate investing and borrowing members, rapidly evolved.

Investors could deposit and withdraw funds. Borrowing members were granted loans, repayable with interest over a set number of years. And since societies no longer had to terminate once all founder members had received their share of the accumulated funds, the way was also open for the longer-term expansion of individual permanent societies. First recorded in 1845, permanent societies rapidly expanded in number and grew in size, soon outstripping the original 'terminators', which died off early this century.

Many present day societies can in fact be traced back to the earliest permanent societies, and it was the development of permanent societies that really marked the origins of the modern building society movement. As an 1872 Royal Commission put it, the growth of the permanent societies 'altogether changed the character and altered the sphere of the building society movement.'

There were three important changes. First, societies rapidly took on their modern character of *financial* institutions, albeit specialised on the lending side in the housing sector. In fact, to the Royal Commission, they appeared little different in some respects from banks. They appeared to be 'mainly agencies for the investment of capital, rather than for enabling the industrious to provide dwellings for themselves'.

Second, the term 'building society' was already largely an historical curiosity. Again in the words of the Commissioners, then, as now: 'Building societies do not build, they simply make advances on building. They are in fact investment associations, mainly confining themselves to real property'. A significant part of their lending was to individuals buying houses for owner occupation. Loans to developers and landlords building or buying houses to rent out were also common, however, and continued into the early 1930s. Lending to landowners, house builders and even, early on, industrialists, was not uncommon.

Third, the management and boards of directors of these rapidly expanding and increasingly complex institutions was soon professionalised, and taken over by the educated bourgeoisie, shaking loose the societies' working class roots.

In the late Victorian period, societies increasingly turned their backs on the demon drink. Some met in the more sober atmosphere of temperance halls and non-conformist school rooms. Others, such as the Halifax, started early on to acquire office premises from which to operate, and the local aristocracy and worthies filled the boardroom. Liberal and non-conformist connections grew. The modern *Building Societies Gazette* received start-up funds from the non-conformist journal *Christian World*.

Much discussion in the Royal Commission Report focused around the issue of whether societies should enjoy some form of legal status as corporate bodies, separate from banks or limited liability companies. Was there any justification for maintaining such distinctions, or could they simply register as a bank or company under the relevant Act?

It was a debate reminiscent in many ways of discussion around the 1986 Act which, among other things, allowed societies to convert to Public Limited Companies. The 1874 Act in fact came out in favour of separate legal status. It made a distinction between the 'mutual' nature of the societies based on 'membership' and the profit-orientated character of banks and companies owned collectively by their shareholders.

It was a dubious distinction at the time. Mass membership permanent societies bore little relationship to the cosy, self-help image of the early organisations. But separate corporate identity served to isolate societies, though not completely, from some of the wilder excesses of the financial and corporate world in the early part of the century and the inter-war period. By focusing building society lending on property, primarily housing, it provided for their growth and stability. This also provided for their unique role as the major source of funding for the massive expansion of owner occupation after the First World War.

As the government's Chief Registrar of Friendly Societies observed on the centenary of the 1874 Act, it 'provided the legal framework within the broad framework of which building societies have operated ever since', or up to 1986 at least. The 1874 Act, as already noted, proved very durable. The development of the societies was by no means smooth. There were supplementary Acts, usually in response to some particular crisis which threatened confidence in 'the movement' as it continued to be called. There was consolidating legislation in 1962. But the original framework proved adequate in broad terms as a basis for the massive modern expansion of the societies — in part because the societies remained, despite this massive growth, relatively simple institutions. They took in funds from investors largely in the form of personal savings. Much of this money was then loaned out long-term to individual house buyers. The remainder was invested in a range of relatively secure public sector stock, providing a cushion of more liquid assets.

Major expansion was not to come until the inter-war period and the first large scale expansion of home ownership in the 1930s. There were early setbacks. In 1892, the massive Liberator Building Society collapsed. Like others at the time, it had loaned heavily to industrial and property companies. Its demise shook confidence in the movement as a whole. This

was not helped by the subsequent collapse in 1911 of the
Birkbeck. This society had invested heavily in gilt-edged stocks
which lost their shine as values tumbled.

By 1919, then, societies still represented relatively minor
players on the national financial scene, but the game-plan had
been drawn up. In 1919, less than one household in ten were
owner occupiers. Eighty per cent rented from private landlords.
By 1990, 66 per cent of households were homeowners. The
massive growth of building societies was a key factor,
inextricably linked with the revolution in housing tenure over
70 years. It was linked not only economically, but politically,
for the societies allied themselves closely with the interests of
home-owners and the expansion of home-ownership as a form
of tenure.

Significantly in this respect, the societies funded not only the
purchase of new housing but also transfers from the private
and, more recently, public rented sectors.

The first real boom in private building came in the early
1930s. Ramsay MacDonald's Tory-dominated 'national
government' abolished subsidies to local authority housing built
to meet general needs. During
this period, moreover, real
incomes of those in
employment were actually
rising, encouraging house
purchase and investment. The
societies experienced a
massive inflow of funds, since
they offered security, liquidity
and high returns compared to
stocks and shares.

House prices, meanwhile,
were static or falling in real
terms. The result was a major
upsurge in private building,
primarily for owner occu-
pation, from around 130,000
in 1931 to an annual average
of 260,000 over the period
1935-39. Alongside this,

Abbey National

Every hour someone buys
a house of their own
through "The National"

NATIONAL HOUSE, MOORGATE, LONDON, E.C.2.   MET.8410

**Early advertising and marketing ideas
from the National Building Society.**

building society funds grew from £87 million in 1920 to £756 million by 1940.

With massive funds to lend, competition between societies grew, and lending practices changed in an attempt to encourage borrowing. Mortgage terms were extended from 15 to 20 years to the now customary 25, or even 30, years. The current practice of lending beyond the usual 70-75 per cent of house values, with the 'excess' being covered by an insurance policy, dates from this period.

Inter-society competition at this time generated increasing problems. One particular scheme involved lending beyond 70-75 per cent of valuation on the basis of deposits from builders, keen to secure loans for those buying their particular houses. This 'builders' pool' system, which became widespread in the 1930s, compounded the problems of downmarket lending on poorer quality housing, as builders sought to cash in on the housing boom.

The famous case of *Bradford Third Equitable Building Society v. Borders* focused attention on deteriorating building standards and the questionable character of the builders' pool. Mrs Borders, whose new house had been particularly badly built, was taken to court by the Society for non-payment. She brought counter claims, which among other things questioned the legality of the builders' pool system. There were more widespread 'mortgage strikes', with several thousand people withholding mortgage payments, until the legality of the pool system was clarified or housing defects were corrected. In response, the 1939 Building Societies Act, one of the supplementary Acts mentioned earlier, attempted to define what represented acceptable security for loans.

After the war, the Labour government's initial commitment to public housing, coupled with retention of the wartime licensing scheme to control private building, at first held down building for owner occupation. With the return of the Conservatives under Macmillan, restrictions on private building were lifted and, subsequently, subsidies for local authority housing for general needs again reduced over a period of time to zero.

Societies' pent-up funds and post-war growth funded the second major surge in building for owner occupation through

the 1950s and 1960s. By the 1970s, the societies had emerged
as a major force in the finance market with collective assets in
the same league as the banks, pension funds and insurance
companies. They were, moreover, the predominant source of
funding for house purchase. Expansion was consolidated
through the 1970s, albeit with an underlying pattern of market
boom and slump. Owner occupation continued to expand. But
pressure was building up in the late 1970s and early 1980s
towards more fundamental change, culminating in the 1986
Act.

Financial deregulation in the UK, plus the transformation of
international finance markets, had major implications for house
purchase finance in general and the societies in particular. Stock
exchange deregulation and the 'big bang', abolition of exchange
controls and the removal of constraints on the commercial
banks were among the key factors behind the much greater
competitive pressures faced by societies in the 1980s. They
experienced mounting competition for personal sector savings
from the banks and other less traditional institutions.

The mortgage market was also radically transformed.
Innovation, and competition, both between societies and with
other institutions, increased. Interest rates were pushed up.
The cartel arrangement which fixed building society interest
rates, and fixed them below what economists call the 'market
clearing rate' at which demand for loans would be fully met,
broke down.

Societies remain the major source of home loans, but banks
and other financial institutions rapidly increased their market
share. And, in contrast to the mortgage rationing of the 1970s,
loans are now freely available at market interest rates. Societies
no longer enjoy a semi-monopoly of the mortgage market.

It was apparent, however, that the capacity of societies to
respond to the increasingly competitive environment of the
1980s and beyond was limited by the existing legislative
framework. Interest rate margins on traditional savings and
home loans were being squeezed in the newly competitive
environment. There was also concern that continued expansion
in the longer term could not simply rely on continued growth
in owner occupation, and that some sort of limit to the
expansion of home ownership would be reached at around

70-75 per cent. Societies saw, on the other hand, increasing commercial opportunities to expand into new areas of activity.

There was mounting pressure, therefore, to widen the scope of building society operations. This culminated in the 1986 Act and related measures. Together, these significantly expanded building society powers and introduced a new supervisory framework. Societies remain centrally concerned with lending for house purchase and related activities. The new legislation has, however, gone a long way towards removing the distinctions between societies and other financial services institutions. They have, moreover, become increasingly integrated into more general financial markets.

The new legislation eased restrictions on the use of funds, allowing for unsecured loans and finance for land and property development. It allowed for diversification into activities related to house purchase and more general financial services — estate agency, insurance broking, surveys, money transmission, share-dealing, fund and unit trust management, foreign exchange services. It formalised and gave wide powers to raise wholesale as opposed to personal sector funds. It also provided a mechanism allowing building societies to convert to public limited companies, with building society investors becoming, in the process, shareholders.

The full implications are only starting to be worked through. The pace of innovation, initially rapid, was slowed by recession in the early 1990s. Societies were, however, increasingly involved in a range of both market and low cost rental housing and shared equity schemes. Partnership schemes with housing associations expanded. A number of societies bought up chains of estate agents. Others acquired insurance companies. The Alliance and Leicester acquired Girobank.

More generally, there was rapid diversification into a wide range of financial services including current account banking, credit cards and personal loans, insurance and insurance-linked products, investment, pensions and personal equity plans and the like. And in July 1990, the Abbey National, with 16 per cent of total building society assets, was the first and, so far the only, society to convert to plc status under the 1986 Act.

Fears have been expressed that societies might be over-reaching themselves, venturing into unknown territory. Fingers were burnt by the ill-timed foray into estate agency just as the housing market went into severe decline. At the same time, mortgage arrears reached an all-time high, causing anxiety for the stability of some smaller societies. The government required societies to set aside more capital to cover the risk of default. And while strenuously emphasising the differences, societies and observers had half an eye on the major collapse of Savings and Loans Associations, the US equivalent of the societies. Coupled with recession, this led to some retrenchment in the early 1990s, emphasising core business. Strategic alliances with other specialist institutions were preferred to 'go-it-alone' innovation.

For the future, the societies are likely to retain their major share of home loans, but with continued innovation and diversification into other activities. They are likely to put their weight, assets and political muscle increasingly behind the expansion of private rented and 'third-sector' housing. The 1989 Housing and Local Government Act is clearly designed to render the local authority sector more residual and drive a proportion of tenants into the arms of the commercial or semi-commercial third sector. Competitive and commercial pressures, however, prevent societies from performing any truly *social* housing role.

More generally, the number of societies will continue to decline through acquisition and merger. In 1980 there were over 270 societies. By 1989 there were 126, with further concentration inevitable. The distinction between societies and other institutions in the financial services sector will become increasingly blurred. The *Building Societies Gazette*, in a bit of new decade crystal ball-gazing in January 1990, was describing the 1990s as the decade in which societies would cease to exist as specific creatures under the law, predicting a mid-decade Banking Act which would give them powers equivalent to commercial banks under the authority of the Bank of England. The 1986 Act could, ironically, be the vehicle for the societies' eventual demise as distinctive financial institutions.

In some ways, the societies leap-frogged the commercial banks. By the early 1990s, and courtesy of the 1986 Act, they were well on the way to being broad-based, commercial, financial services institutions. It is significant that the Abbey

National has not, as yet, been followed down the road of conversion to plc status. There was considerable flexibility built into the 1986 legislation, and some of the restrictions set by the Act were subsequently relaxed. The state of the housing market, fear of takeover and the bad press attracted by the Abbey conversion, moreover, sowed doubt among other potential converts.

The 1986 Act does still set some boundaries on diversification and business options. Societies remain distinctive financial entities, still uniquely specialised in the housing sector. In an increasingly competitive environment, however, we can expect to see further restructuring of the industry, and further diversification once the short-term caution of the early 1990s has been overcome.

(This article was first published in ROOF, May 1990).

Chapter 7

Why council housing?

*Was council housing developed as a response to the
failures of the private market, or did the market fail
because of state interference?*

Peter Kemp

Most accounts of the origins of council housing see the Housing
and Town Planning Act 1919 as the key milestone. This Act
was significant because it introduced Exchequer subsidies for
council housebuilding and was the first to place a duty on local
authorities to survey the housing needs of their districts, and
to submit plans for the provision of houses to remedy shortages.

Although a few local authorities had begun to build
unsubsidised rented housing towards the end of the 19th
century, by 1914 only about 24,000 dwellings had been
constructed, mostly by the large city councils. But immediately
after the First World War, the government exhorted local
authorities to build as many 'homes fit for heroes' as they could
manage. By 1939, aided by Exchequer subsidies, they had built
a million homes, accounting for 10 per cent of the total stock
and had become firmly established as housing providers.

Thus the 1919 Act was certainly an important turning point
in the history of council housing. But why did this change of
direction occur? As with so many other areas of our history,
this is under dispute. And nor is this simply a matter of
academic pedantry, for the conclusions one can draw from this

are relevant to current debates about who should provide rented housing.

Some historians have seen the origins of council housing in the Victorian public health reform 'movement', believing it to be a natural and logical progression from that early legislation to do with sanitation, building standards, overcrowding and slum clearance. Council housing was thus one more step on the way to a more enlightened and humane social policy, a product of the growing awareness of bad housing conditions and, ultimately, a recognition of the need to provide decent, subsidised housing to rent for the poor. In this view, local authorities were the obvious candidates for the task of providing housing, since they were already responsible for public health and building regulations.

This 'whig' interpretation of history usually focuses on major Acts of Parliament and on key individuals (usually male, often wealthy) whose foresight and humanity allowed them to be prime movers behind legislation enacted for the benefit of the poor. Indeed, the legislation is often referred to by the names of these 'great men'. Thus the 1919 Act is often called the Addison Act, after the minister responsible for piloting it through Parliament.

In recent years, this somewhat naive view of the inevitability of (subsidised) council housing has been challenged by accounts that focus less on the good deeds of key individuals and more on social forces and conflicts. And instead of being regarded as passive recipients, ordinary women and men are often seen as having had a pivotal role. Moreover, it is argued that there was nothing inevitable about the introduction of Exchequer subsidies for council housing, rather that it needs to be explained and not simply assumed.

At the risk of over-simplification, two competing explanations of the origins of subsidised council housing can be identified. Within each can be identified numerous variations, qualifications and subtleties, but there is insufficient space to consider them here. In brief, the first explanation sees council housing as a *response* to the failure of the private market. The other says the market failed *because* of state interference and that far from being a solution, council housing was part of the problem.

The first view, then, sees the introduction of subsidised council housing as a response to the failure of the private landlord to provide decent quality housing at rents that working people could afford. Some authors focus on the long term failure of the private landlord, while others also argue that there was a permanent, structural, pre-war collapse of investment in private housing to rent which forced the state to intervene in housing provision.

Prior to 1914, perhaps 90 per cent of housing was provided by private landlords, while rents were set by the interaction of supply and demand. Many poor people lived in appalling slum conditions, largely because that was all they could afford. While the introduction of minimum building standards and public health legislation did improve the quality of new construction, it also raised building costs and hence rents. Essentially, the problem was that many people's incomes were simply too low for them to afford decent housing.

It was to show that private enterprise really could provide decent housing at affordable rents that the 'model dwelling companies' were set up in the late 19th century. These forerunners of the housing association movement, such as Peabody and Guinness, constructed blocks of dwellings and aimed to give five per cent return to their investors, compared with the eight per cent often secured on rented housing at that time. Yet their rents were usually still too high for the poorest households, and the dwellings were often let to the better-off working class.

This was also true of the (unsubsidised) housing built by local authorities before 1914; it was generally beyond the means of the poorest households. Moreover, like the model dwelling companies' housing, it was often aimed at those considered to be the 'deserving poor' anyway, not those whom we would now regard as being most in need. Prior to 1914 a debate did emerge about whether local authorities should get more involved in providing rented housing. But even many of those in favour of subsidies for council housing saw local authorities as taking second place to the private sector, perhaps filling gaps in provision and providing a model with which the market could compete.

Sylva cottages in 1890 — 24 three room dwellings built by the London County Council in south London.

Some versions of the market failure explanation claim there was a collapse of investment in rented housing before 1914, which signalled an end to private landlordism. Hence the introduction of subsidies for council housing was a necessary consequence of this crisis. On this view, the war merely influenced the timing of the introduction of subsidies, while rent controls were only another nail in the private landlord's coffin rather than the fatal blow.

An alternative explanation sees council housing as a consequence of the First World War. On this view, the pre-war slump of investment in rented housing construction was essentially a cyclical downturn rather than permanent collapse, one from which it would have recovered had it not been for the introduction of rent controls in 1915 following rent strikes in Glasgow and elsewhere.

The introduction of Exchequer subsidies in 1919 is seen, in this view, as a direct consequence of rent controls. Politically, the housing shortage made it imperative that building took place after the war, yet it also made it impossible to remove rent controls. And unless rent controls were removed, private landlords would not build any houses, especially as building costs and interest rates had increased greatly during the war. Hence an emergency programme of subsidised council house-building had to be introduced to remove the shortage, thus making it possible to end rent controls and get the building of housing to rent back onto a commercial footing.

The subsequent failure to decontrol rents meant that private investment in rented housing never returned and council housing has remained with us ever since. For some, this transformation amounted to the 'sacrifice' of the private landlord, representing (for those on the left) a notable victory for working class struggle or (for those on the right) a lack of political will to implement decontrol.

In trying to make sense of these competing explanations it is helpful to distinguish between two separate (though related) questions. First, why did the government introduce housing subsidies in 1919 when previously it had been most reluctant to do so? Second, why were local authorities given the subsidies and entrusted with responsibility for the housing programme? For in other countries, as Milner Holland pointed out in 1964, subsidies were focused on private landlords and housing associations, while municipal housing was given a relatively minor role.

Separating these issues makes it easier to understand why subsidies were introduced. The failure of the private sector to provide decent quality housing for the poorest households created growing pressures on government to do something about the housing question. The pre-war decade did see a major, though not a complete, collapse of investment in rented housing and this made some kind of state intervention very likely. Indeed, there is evidence to suggest that the war may have delayed the introduction of Exchequer subsidies. Even so, we do not know for sure what the precise nature and scale of the subsidy would eventually have been.

In the event, the war transformed the whole way in which the housing question was debated. First, the severe housing shortage that developed during the war and the social unrest this threatened made it urgent that the state deal with it when war ended. The short-term increase in building costs and interest rates meant that, unaided, the private sector could not be relied upon to meet the shortage. Some kind of subsidy, therefore, was even more necessary to ensure that building took place in the immediate post-war period than it had been before 1914.

Secondly, the war had a significant effect upon the way in which assistance was provided, with the result that local authorities emerged as the obvious candidates to carry out the postwar building programme. The wartime rent strikes and profiteering by some private landlords meant that, politically, it was not possible to give subsidies to private landlords. Though never popular, private landlords became widely reviled during and after the war, and this effectively precluded them from receiving handouts from the state. However, an additional Housing Act passed towards the end of 1919 did provide grants to private housebuilders.

Housing associations (or 'public utility societies' as they were known) were considered for the job of meeting the postwar housing shortage, but were not felt able to cope with the scale of the problem. Even so, the Addison Act of 1919 did make subsidies available to them on a similar basis to local authority building. The societies eventually constructed 4,545 dwellings under the Act, compared with 170,000 by local authorities, in England and Wales.

It was also considered whether central government itself should carry out the programme, but this course was rejected because the Ministry of Works did not have the necessary local knowledge. Local authorities did have knowledge of local housing market conditions, land supply and building costs. And unlike the public utility societies they collectively covered the whole country. Moreover, local councils already had building and other housing powers under pre-war legislation and hence some relevant experience. Furthermore, state housing was a demand of several groups representing working people at this time, while a number of official reports — including the Royal Commission on Scottish Housing, which was set up before the war but reported in 1917 — recommended that subsidies for municipal housing be introduced.

Yet many local authorities were initially reluctant to get involved in providing housing, especially if it meant a charge on the rates. This was partly why the 1919 Act subsidy was so generous: all their deficits above the product of a penny rate (4/5d in Scotland) were met by the Exchequer. Despite this open-ended subsidy, the rents charged on 1919 Act houses were too high for many working class tenants, and they were often let to better-off and lower middle class households. Some councils even had to advertise their larger houses outside of the district in order to find tenants for them.

During 1919-20, the Ministry of Health urged authorities to build as many houses as they could and gave advice on design as well as construction materials and methods to hasten the implementation of the programme. Yet in 1921 the subsidies were prematurely axed. This is used by one commentator, Mark Swenarton, to justify his argument that the 'homes fit for heroes' campaign was designed as an insurance against revolution, aimed at buying off social unrest. Once the threat of revolution had receded, the insurance policy was no longer needed and could be terminated, especially in view of its high cost.

Cabinet minutes show that fear of revolution was certainly a significant factor behind the post-war housing programme, but Swenarton's case is too crude. In any case, it does not explain why subsidies were re-introduced (for private and municipal house-building) by the Conservatives in 1923. This was due to the growing housing shortage and the failure of the private sector to build many houses. The Labour government which briefly came to power in 1924 also introduced a subsidy — for municipal and private rented construction — which resulted in half a million council houses being built, compared with 75,000 under the less generous 1923 Act.

When the Conservatives returned to power in late 1924, they retained Labour's subsidy along with their own of 1923. While their legislation gave council housing only a residual role, Labour's 1924 Act orientated councils towards meeting general needs; the Conservatives were 'reluctant collectivists' who supported this tenure largely because investment in privately rented construction had dried up and alternatives had to be found, while Labour favoured municipal provision.

It was the 1924 Act, rather than that of 1919, which really established council housing as a long-term feature of the housing market. It had little to do with slogans about 'homes for heroes', however, and instead reflected the collapse of private rental construction. Criticised in a Commons debate for interfering with private housing investment, Labour's Minister of Health, John Wheatley, pointed out that there was no investment in working class homes. 'Are we to remain without houses,' he replied, 'merely because people who have money . . . refuse to invest that money directly in working class houses?'

Some would say the lack of investment in private rented building after the war was due to the failure to decontrol rents. But rent control applied only to pre-1919 dwellings, not to new build. Economic factors were more important, especially the dramatic increase in building costs at the end of the war and the (correct) expectation that they would eventually fall. Hence investing in rented housing would have meant making a capital loss when house prices eventually fell.

In the 1930s, when housing market conditions had improved, a revival of building for private rental (averaging over 66,000 units a year in 1933-39) did occur, but by then council housing and owner occupation had become established as powerful competitors to the private landlord, as indeed they still are.

(This article was first published in ROOF, March 1989).

Chapter 8

Investment strategies

Compared to the current complex rules on finance for council housing, most subsidy systems in operation since 1919 were models of simplicity.

Peter Malpass

For more than 70 years, successive British governments have been drawn into repeated bouts of legislation on council house subsidies. The latest example, the Local Government and Housing Act 1989, represents the nineteenth housing subsidies act since 1919, and the Conservatives' second attempt to reform the system since they took power in 1979.

The frequency of legislation on housing subsidies in the council sector is not just a reflection of party differences. A switch in the reasonably near future seems to be historically inevitable, whichever party is in power.

In view of all the practice that civil servants have had in devising subsidy systems over the years, it might be argued that, by the late 1980s, they should have been able to come up with something capable of surviving more than just a few years.

After all, housing association subsidies are not changed with anything like the same frequency, and the system of financial support for owner occupiers is easy to comprehend and hardly ever changed. In the case of council housing, however, complexity seems to increase as one subsidy regime replaces another. By comparison with the 1989 Act system, the majority of subsidy systems operated since 1919 represent models of simplicity.

The first housing subsidy category can be described as investment subsidy, where the local authority was given a fixed cash sum, per dwelling, per year, for a specified period of years. The term *investment subsidy* is used because the subsidy was related to an authority's investment in *new* building, and represented a contribution towards loan charges arising from that new building.

The second category is *deficit subsidy*, which is based on the overall balance between income and expenditure in the housing revenue account (HRA).

The third category is *rent rebate subsidy*, and is different in certain important respects from the first two, mainly because it is calculated according to the incomes of individual tenants and because it can exist alongside both investment and deficit subsidy, whereas they are mutually exclusive categories.

Historically, large scale investment in council housing was launched in 1919 on the basis of a deficit subsidy system, which was very soon abandoned in favour of a succession of investment subsidy systems over the following 50 years.

It is only since 1972 that governments have returned to versions of deficit subsidy, and only in this period, too, that they have provided an explicit rent rebate subsidy. This prompts questions about why deficit subsidy was first adopted, only to be abandoned, and why the principle has been revived in recent times.

At the end of the First World War, building costs were very high, and rents could not cover expenditure on loan charges, and management and maintenance. Under the 1919 Act, the local authorities' liability to contribute to income deficits was limited to the product of a penny rate, and the Exchequer made up the rest. This arrangement suited the local authorities, but left the Exchequer exposed to an open ended liability, a situation which highlights a basic feature of deficit subsidy systems: who decides the size of the deficit?

Central government was naturally inclined to be suspicious that local authorities would adopt extravagant building standards, but would set low rents. Even where authorities set modest standards, the system put no pressure on them to be efficient and scrupulous about containing costs.

In practice, the Ministry of Health set up an elaborate administrative apparatus, based on 11 regional offices, designed to monitor and control local authority behaviour. Where rents were deemed to be too low, subsidy could be withheld, subject to appeal to a tribunal. The city of Bristol, for instance, was faced with loss of subsidy after deciding in 1920 to reduce rents because they were beyond the reach of many families on the waiting list.[1]

Eventually the tribunal ruled in the city's favour and the subsidy was paid, but this illustration shows how deficit subsidy systems complicate the relationship between central and local government. The essential point is that although local authorities incur the costs and set the rents, the central government covers the deficit and therefore has a close interest in the relationship between income and expenditure.

Central government escaped from the complexities of deficit subsidy by adopting the investment subsidy model in 1923. The Housing Act 1923 established a system which said that in future, new building by local authorities would attract a subsidy of £6 per dwelling, per year, for 20 years.

The Labour government of 1924 introduced a higher rate of Exchequer subsidy, payable over a longer period, and in view of contemporary central government attitudes to subsidy and to new house-building by councils, it is interesting to note the nature of the bargaining over the subsidy level at that time. The government wanted houses to be built, and the authorities were in a strong position to negotiate subsidy.

The Labour Minister of Health, John Wheatley, reported to the House of Commons that the local authorities had pressed for £12 per house and that: 'It was only at the very last moment, by a very strong appeal to the local authorities, that they agreed to accept £9.'[2]

The 1924 Act reintroduced the notion of a mandatory rate fund contribution (RFC), and this remained a feature of all subsequent Acts until 1956. In addition, authorities were permitted to make discretionary RFCs and were *required* to make an RFC to balance the account if there remained a deficit at the end of the financial year.

Thus, the open ended responsibility for dealing with deficits lay at the local level throughout the period from 1923 to 1972. They could choose to remove deficits by either raising rents or making an RFC, but the requirement was that one way or another the HRA should balance each year.

There were several features of the investment subsidy approach which enabled it to survive for so long. First, it proved to be an effective way of stimulating housing production, and sustained the growth of council housing during periods when policy favoured high output, in the 1950s and 1960s.

Secondly, it gave central government some leverage on the amount and type of new building; the centre was able to raise or lower output according to the incentive provided by the value of subsidy, and it was able to influence the balance between building for general needs and slum clearance.

Thirdly, fixed annual subsidies appealed to the Treasury because they meant that its financial liability was capped and predictable each year.

Fourthly, the system gave local authorities considerable autonomy over such key aspects of housing policy as rents, management and maintenance expenditure and the size of their capital programmes. Councils had an incentive to control costs, because increased costs would not be reflected in higher Exchequer subsidy.

Fifthly, central government could influence local authority rents by means of financial leverage, but without formally breaching local autonomy in the matter. This became important from the mid-1950s, when the government adopted rent pooling as a device for levering rents upwards.

A product of the commitment to fixed annual subsidies was that successive systems were rather crude and insensitive to local cost variations. There were attempts in various Acts to differentiate subsidy levels according to urban or rural location, or, later, for high land costs, but the categories were widely drawn and the outcome was that subsidy was not closely related to local circumstances. In addition, because authorities had control of capital investment for many years there emerged a pattern of wide variation in loan charges, reflecting different rates of building at different times. This in turn influenced rents and levels of RFCs.

By the late 1960s, critics of prevailing policies on rents and subsidies were arguing that council rents generally were too low and that rent setting was approached from the wrong direction. The gradual spread of 'fair' rents in the private sector after the Rent Act 1965 began to change the longstanding pattern in which council rents had usually exceeded controlled private sector rents.

The fact that council subsidies were fixed cash amounts meant that rents tended to be set in terms of what was needed to bridge the gap between subsidy and expenditure, and this might bear little relation to what houses were actually worth, given the impact of inflation. Subsidies were also inequitably distributed amongst local authorities and their tenants.

The outcome of this sort of critique was a package of proposals based on fair rents (setting rents in accordance with current value), deficit subsidy and a separate rent rebate system. These proposals were, however, politically unacceptable to the Labour government in the late 1960s. Fair rents implied a complete removal of local autonomy in rent setting, and implied very large increases for some authorities. Deficit subsidy approaches permit negative subsidies, or HRA surpluses, in certain circumstances, and Labour opposed the idea of 'profits' from council housing.

The government therefore held out against reform, but it did begin another policy trend which has been highly significant in subsequent developments. Economic difficulties in 1967 led the government to cut back on the party's long established commitment to high levels of council house building, and in retrospect 1968 can be seen as marking the end of the high output phase of post-war British housing policy.

The Conservative government which took office in 1970 enthusiastically embraced both lower building rates and the reform of rents and subsidies policy. The Housing Finance Act 1972 was a mould-breaking event — it marked the end of 50 years of continuity around forms of investment subsidy. But it was a seriously flawed measure, both technically and politically. The emphasis in the Act was on rents rather than subsidies, following the logic that rents should be set first so that need for subsidy could then be calculated. Local authorities were instructed to raise rents by annual instalments until fair rent levels were reached, but, unlike previous measures, the 1972 Act contained no financial measures to ensure that authorities did what they were told.

The 1970s represented a period of digression from, and reversion to, financial leverage on local authority rents. The 1972 Act was the digression, which was repealed in 1975 and replaced by a temporary measure, pending creation of a more permanent solution. However, some important developments did take place at that time. In particular a broad consensus was established around the idea that council rents should reflect the *current value* of money rather than historic costs, and that there should be a separate rent rebate system to channel assistance to people in greatest need.

Another important development of the 1970s, implemented in the 1980s, was the notional housing revenue account as the basis for subsidy payments. The notional HRA combines elements of central control and local autonomy, and, like pre-1972 systems, relies on financial leverage as the means of applying central pressure on rents.

After the political difficulties encountered in the early 1970s, arising from attempts to instruct local authorities to raise rents, the Housing Act 1980 reverted to a system of setting subsidy first and letting councils make the subsequent rents decisions. The 1980 system was clearly influenced by the need to accommodate a degree of local autonomy in rent setting, but at the same time it was a policy driven more by subsidy considerations than a concern about rent levels.

It is in the nature of deficit subsidy systems that the legislation specifies ways of calculating assistance rather than stating amounts of entitlement. But this inevitably clouds the situation for local authorities, who are left with no certainty about movements in subsidy from year to year.

The 1980 Act contained a formula for the calculation of subsidy, based on the amount paid in the previous year and notional changes in income and expenditure (principally income from rents and expenditure on management and maintenance). Each year the secretary of state issued two 'determinations', representing his assumptions about changes in rents and management and maintenance (M&M)

expenditure. The amount of leverage on rents depended upon the size of the gap between these two determinations.

In practice, the secretary of state tended to assume that rents would rise faster than M&M expenditure, and most authorities experienced sharp cut-backs in subsidy, especially at first. In aggregate terms the amount of deficit subsidy fell by over 80 per cent in the first three years that the system was in operation, and by the late 1980s, four out of five authorities were no longer receiving Housing Act subsidy (but they were all receiving rent rebate subsidy).

The effect of the leverage approach to raising rents meant that rents could only be driven upwards by the centre if it was assumed that M&M expenditure rose more slowly than rent income, and therefore that increases in rent were reflected in lower subsidy rather than improved services to tenants. In this sense, the government became the agent of disrepair in the public sector.

Calculation of actual subsidy on the basis of a notional HRA was, then, a way of both capping Exchequer liability for deficit subsidy and a way of keeping rents rising. It was also a way of shifting the balance between deficit and rebate subsidy, and the consequences of this aspect of the system finally led to its downfall. The 1980 Act system was designed for a period of stock *contraction* rather than growth, and for the new era of HRA surpluses, rather than deficits.

A system based on current value rents and deficit subsidy implies, especially in periods of price inflation and low investment, that deficits will disappear and surpluses will arise. The issues, then, are: who determines the size of surpluses, how are they made actual rather than notional, and who has the right to dispose of them?

A further problem arises in the context of systems such as the 1980 Act approach to rent setting: central government pressure can only be put on rents by reducing the size of notional deficits, and once deficits disappear, authorities regain much greater autonomy.

The leverage approach adopted in 1980 can be seen as a direct response to the difficulties of *instructing* authorities to raise rents in 1972, and in their design, the architects of the 1980 system recognised the problem of dealing with surpluses.

Essentially what they did was to design the method of calculating rate support grant (in the Local Government, Planning and Land Act 1980) in such a way that authorities with *notional* HRA surpluses could be put under pressure to make those *actual* surpluses and to transfer them to the general rate fund.

In practice this mechanism was used only once, in 1981/82, and then abandoned because of political opposition from Conservative-controlled local authorities. The outcome was that well over a quarter of all authorities soon moved into surplus, thereby subsidising the rates.

The new financial regime was devised in the late 1980s to overcome what central government saw as unreasonably high levels of subsidy to council housing. On the one hand, it was paying rent rebate subsidy to more than 100 authorities where the HRA was actually in surplus, and, on the other hand, another group of authorities were seen to be 'indiscriminately' subsidising council housing through rate fund contributions.

The ringfence around the HRA is designed to remove 'excess' rebate and subsidy and RFCs. The incorporation of rebate subsidy into the new HRA subsidy can be seen in terms of the government's need to give itself renewed leverage on rents, whilst preserving an element of local control over rents. The problem, however, is that the centre has gone beyond the ringfence and has introduced new areas of complexity in the form of much more sophisticated approaches to assessing changes in rents and M&M expenditure.

The history of British council housing subsidy systems provides a way of explaining the complexity of the new regime. The current system is very much a product of its antecedents. For many years, subsidy policy was about giving incentives to build, and the *pattern* of building was perhaps less important to governments than the aggregate level of output.

The old subsidy systems were simple but crude, making very little allowance for local cost variations. However, they did allow local autonomy and included the important safety valve of discretionary RFCs. Nevertheless, wide variations in costs of new development and the level of debt charges per dwelling generated significant variations in rents.

A major proportion of the difficulty now facing policy makers is due to the *laissez-faire* attitudes of the past. Not only were authorities free to set their own investment levels, but also their own administrative structures and accounting conventions.

In an inflationary environment, governments will naturally want to keep rents on the move, irrespective of ideological preferences for public or private housing. In the 1950s and 1960s, the rate of new building, and therefore the rate of debt expansion, made it possible to lever rents upwards by underfunding new building and relying on rent pooling to raise rents for all. But in an era of disinvestment, things are not so simple, because the government is trying to cut new building, increase rents, recoup surpluses and generally restrict local autonomy.

Notes

1. M Daunton (Ed), *Councillors and tenants: local authority housing in English cities 1919-1939*, Leicester University Press, 1984, pp.198-9.
2. *House of Commons debates* Vol 175, June 1924, Col 102.

(This article was first published in ROOF in July 1991, and updated in December 1991).

Chapter 9

Rents within reach

The argument about 'bricks and mortar' subsidies versus income subsidies for poorer tenants has its origins in the early days of rent rebate schemes and the fierce political debates they provoked.

Peter Malpass

At the present time, 60 per cent of council tenants rely on housing benefit to help them pay their rent, and the idea of rent rebates to assist those on low incomes is a very well established feature of housing policy in all rented sectors. But it was not always like this.

The provision of rebates on a large scale is a relatively modern development — as recently as 20 years ago less than ten per cent of council tenants received rebates, and only since 1972 have local authorities been required to provide rebates for low income tenants.

The origins of housing benefit lie in debates 60 years ago about the proper way to distribute housing subsidy. The argument was over whether subsidies were intended to reduce the standard rents for all houses, irrespective of the incomes of individual tenants, or to be restricted to those tenants who qualified for help on grounds of low income. This came to be expressed as a debate about subsidies for 'bricks and mortar' or for 'people', but it is really about pricing policy and the relationship between housing and social security.

The idea of providing rent rebates emerged in the late 1920s, after a decade of housing subsidies, which had been introduced in order to regenerate house-building after the First World War. In the immediate aftermath of the war, housing construction costs rose to several times their pre-war level, and without subsidy, the rents of new houses would have been well beyond the reach of working class families, even those on relatively high earnings.

Although costs soon fell away from their 1920 peak, the 1920s as a whole can be seen as a decade of relatively high house prices and interest rates. In this context, it was accepted that general assistance was appropriate, and subsidies were provided for private builders as well as local authorities.

However, towards the end of the decade, the situation began to look rather different and new arguments emerged. Prices were falling, which meant the possibility of a viable market for unsubsidised new private housing for the rather better-off workers. It was also becoming clear that a decade of housing subsidies had been of very little benefit to the least well-off; despite subsidies, rents in many areas had remained too high for council housing to be affordable by the poor.

And by 1929, politicians were turning their attention to the problem of a century of virtually unregulated urban housing development for the industrial working class: the 'slums' were once again on the political agenda, and it was recognised that any programme of slum clearance would involve the rehousing of large numbers of poor families.

The response of the Conservative government in the late 1920s was to encourage local authorities to take advantage of falling prices, and lower standards, in order to channel new houses to lower income families at rents below those set for earlier houses. The Tories also went into the 1929 general election with a policy of 'reconditioning' the slums rather than demolishing them.

However, a minority Labour government was elected, and the new Minister of Health, Arthur Greenwood, brought forward a Bill designed to launch a national programme of slum clearance. The Bill contained proposals for a new subsidy, specifically related to the number of people rehoused from slum clearance. This was to exist alongside the 1924 Act subsidy for 'general needs housing'. The slum clearance subsidy was presented as more generous than the general needs subsidy, but the Bill contained no mechanisms to ensure that the recipients of this extra help were those who actually needed it.

Although the text books generally report that the Housing Act 1930 introduced rent rebates, it is important to note that it was not the policy of the Labour government at that time to encourage rebating. In fact the freedom for local authorities to provide rent rebate schemes was introduced into the Bill at a late stage in its passage through Parliament, and as a result of backbench pressure rather than government initiative. Both Labour and Conservative politicians in those days were generally opposed to the principle of rent rebates, albeit for different reasons.

Labour's opposition rested on its wider distaste for means testing, while for the Tories the objection was that rebates in effect represented a subsidy to employers paying low wages.

The campaign for rent rebates was led by Eleanor Rathbone, who sat as an Independent MP for the English Universities between 1929 and 1946, supported by Sir Ernest Simon, Liberal member for Manchester Withington between 1929 and 1931.

Eleanor Rathbone's greatest achievement was her role in the establishment of family allowances in 1945. As early as 1924 she set up the Family Endowment Society to campaign for family allowances, and its influence was brought to bear in the cause of rent rebates too. In her early advocacy of rebates, Rathbone referred to them as 'children's rent rebates'. Her argument was that rent paying capacity was related to the number of dependents in a family, hence the view that if subsidies were to be available in council housing, they should take account of different household circumstances.

In her maiden speech in the House of Commons, Rathbone went straight into an attack on general subsidy: 'It would have been far better if the local authorities had fixed the rents — I know I am enunciating a heresy in the view of most people here — at the economic value of the house, and had then used the subsidy according to principles clearly laid down and carefully thought out, to relieve the needs of those who most needed housing relief.'[1]

In the debates on the 1930 Housing Bill, Eleanor Rathbone and Sir Ernest Simon argued their case in the face of official indifference and opposition. Simon himself described their battle in these words: 'Miss Rathbone and I fought hard during the various stages of the Greenwood Bill to secure an amendment to the effect that the subsidies should only be given to those who need them and only for so long as they need them; in other words, that the subsidy should be attached to the tenant and not to the house. Mr Greenwood resisted our amendments, but did ultimately accept amendments to the effect that, although the local authority was not compelled to confine the subsidy to those who need them, it was at least authorised to do so.'[2] This account is substantially corroborated by Eleanor Rathbone's biographers.[3]

Thus it was that the Housing Act 1930 gave a power for councils to grant rent rebates, on such terms and conditions as they thought fit. What was to become the major form of rent assistance half a century later actually began as a reluctant concession to a couple of troublesome backbenchers in 1930.

There was no compulsion on local authorities, there were no guidelines as to how rebate schemes might be designed and implemented, nor was the power to provide rebates extended beyond those dwellings built under the 1930 Act. It was clear from the way in which Greenwood referred to Labour's rents policy that the government did not envisage a rebating approach. He was still talking about using the new subsidy to provide some houses at lower rents, rather than rebates for specific *tenants*.

After the fall of the Labour government in 1931, the new national government, dominated by Conservatives, continued the lukewarm line on rebates. For the Tories, the preferred route to lower rents for the poor was still lower standards. However, the Housing Act 1935 introduced the requirement that local authorities should maintain a single housing revenue account for all their houses and flats, and this opened up the possibility of rent rebate schemes which were applicable across the whole stock.

It is hardly surprising in view of the attitude of successive governments in the 1930s, that the local authorities on the whole made little use of their power to introduce rebate schemes. They had reasons of their own for not being enthusiastic about rebates. The provision of rebates implies a commitment to poor families, but local authorities generally seem to have been unwilling to give preference to such families.

This was pointed out by Simon in 1933 when he wrote that not only were the 1924 Act houses too expensive for the lower paid, but also local authorities had not gone out of their way to make these houses available to those in greatest need. 'Unfortunately, although the local authorities have generally passed resolutions in favour of housing large families, those who have administered the letting of the houses have tended to give the first chance to "good" tenants, that is to say, those with a fair income and few children.'[4]

Apart from their attitude to tenants, local authorities had other reasons for being wary of rent rebate schemes. Given the lack of advice and guidance from central government, local councils adopting the idea of rebating found themselves entering an uncharted area, full of administrative, financial and political difficulties. In addition to the complexity of a scheme which varied rents according to household composition and/or income, there was the problem of monitoring changes of circumstances and keeping the rents actually charged in line with such changes. All this meant an increased workload for the housing management staff.

However, perhaps of greater significance was the problem of designing a feasible scheme. What the authorities had to do was use the Exchequer subsidy, which was paid in the form of a fixed sum per house, per year, as a pool from which to pay needs-related rebates. This meant taking subsidy that was paid for one purpose and redistributing it for another. The subsidy pool was finite, although it could be topped up from local rates income, and the problem was to decide how much of that pool to allocate to rebates, and then to construct an income scale of need and a benefit scale which would fit together in such a way that the level of demand did not drain the pool too quickly. The penalty for miscalculation would be either a scheme which failed to provide adequate help for those in need, or which was so generous that funds ran out and ratepayers had to be asked to balance the account.

Then there was the opposition of tenants themselves. During the 1930s, rent rebate schemes proved to be highly unpopular with existing tenants, partly because of the redistribution of subsidy which was required. The use of housing subsidy as a rebates pool required that the benefit of subsidy had to be reduced or withheld altogether from the more affluent tenants.

To introduce a rebate scheme into an existing stock of houses therefore required rent *increases* for some at the same time as reductions for others. The better-off tenants were thus being asked, in a sense, to subsidise the reduced rents of their poorer neighbours. It is easy to see that this could generate considerable resentment amongst the better-off, with the threat of political unpopularity and even electoral defeat for the councillors responsible.

It is important to remember that in the 1920s it had been necessary for tenants to show that they earned enough to afford the rent of a new council house. But in the rather different climate of the 1930s their affluence was turned against them; the London County Council actually wrote to 300 tenants on two estates in 1934 suggesting that they no longer needed subsidised housing and should leave. It must have seemed very unfair to these people, who had been selected precisely because they were deemed to be able to pay the rent for a new council house, now to find that they were expected to give up their home for tenants who could not afford the full rent.

Attempts to persuade better-off tenants to leave were in fact rare, but raising their rents in order to give rebates to the poor must have spurred some to opt for alternatives, such as home-ownership, which experienced a boom in the mid-1930s. Council housing had acquired a rather privileged status in the early post-war years, accommodating the better-off skilled workers and the self-consciously respectable working class. Rent rebate schemes represented a threat to their position, not just because of the increase in rent but because of the accompanying influx of the less well-off and less respectable elements of the working class. Council housing in the 1930s was under attack; on the one hand there was the criticism that affluence was being unjustly subsidised, while on the other hand the extension of subsidy to the poor led to allegations of 'coals in the bath' behaviour by the undeserving poor who did not know how to live in decent housing.

In practice most local authorities avoided any entanglement with rent rebates, and even the recently formed Central Housing Advisory Committee in the first report of its housing management committee in 1939 expressly avoided discussion of what it called the 'controversial question' of rebates. This report stated that only 80 local authorities (out of over 1400) operated formal rent rebate schemes, although others were prepared to give rebates on merit.

In Scotland, the Department of Health pursued a rather more enthusiastic line than the Ministry of Health in England and Wales, and there was more local interest north of the border.

Those few authorities that did introduce rebate schemes tended to confine them to tenants rehoused from slum clearance areas under the Housing Act 1930. Despite the small number of schemes, the variety was immense. At one extreme was the Middlesbrough scheme of 'rent differentiation', which attempted to grade houses and tenants in such a way that 'grade A' houses (nearest the shops and private residential areas) were let at the full economic rent to the highest paid tenants, while 'grade C' houses were allocated to the poor at low rents.

At the opposite extreme was the Leeds scheme which incorporated the entire housing stock (except the 1919 Act houses which were excluded for legal reasons). This scheme involved distributing subsidy in such a way that large families on low incomes could qualify for a nil rent assessment. Most other schemes involved setting a standard rent as the starting point for rebates, and they often included a minimum charge beyond which no rebate could be provided however low the tenant's income.

The experience of Leeds city council probably acted as a warning to many other authorities and it is worth expanding a little on what happened there. In April 1934 the Labour-controlled council introduced a scheme in which all subsidy was drawn into the rent rebate pool, and full economic rents were set for all houses. This meant increases on the basic rent of 70-100 per cent, before calculation of rebates according to family income and needs. The rebates resulted in some tenants paying no rent at all, while others on higher incomes paid a proportion of the full rent and some received no rebate at all. Thus there was a group of tenants who were much worse off as a result of the scheme's generosity to others.

The political risks were obvious: 'Given the social composition of council estates in the early 1930s, before slum clearance was in full swing, it was inevitable that a scheme which provided for certain tenants to live rent free, and in effect extended a means test to households not applying for public assistance but merely seeking to avoid higher rents, would alienate both the tenants and public opinion in general.'[5]

The rent rebate scheme was bitterly opposed by tenants and there were threats of rent strikes, but in the end the tenants' association fought the issue through the courts, and lost. However, it was also opposed through the ballot box and was held to be a major factor in Labour's defeat in the 1935 municipal elections.

Another example of the bitterness generated by rent rebate schemes in the 1930s was the proposal by the Conservative-controlled Birmingham city council in 1939. This was an attempt to drive better-off tenants out of council housing and to remove similar applicants from the waiting list in order that the city could proceed with meeting the enormous need arising from slum clearance. Again it was the introduction of a means test which aroused most opposition, but in this case there was a prolonged rent strike by over 7,000 tenants. The approach of the Second World War overshadowed these events and when the war started the rebate plan was dropped.[6]

By the end of the 1930s the idea of rent rebates was looking like a failed experiment — unpopular with governments, local authorities and tenants alike. It remained a very marginal feature of local authority housing provision, in terms of the number of schemes, the proportion of tenants in any area who benefited and the amount of subsidy diverted into the rebate pool. Underlying the debate about rebating was confusion over the distinction between housing subsidy which is paid as part of a general pricing policy, and income-related assistance which is part of social security policy. Housing subsidy implicitly reflects the view that *landlords* should be paid a form of compensation in order to reduce prices below what they would otherwise be. A rebate is in effect a payment to *tenants* to enable them to afford the rent set by the landlord.

This latter point is more easily grasped in relation to the private rented sector, where it is clearly understood that landlords set rents in accordance with the market value of their properties, rather than the circumstances of individual tenants. The purpose of housing benefit is to ensure that those tenants can afford the rent set by the landlord, and therefore it is clearly the case that tailoring rents to individual tenants' needs is not a landlord activity.

In the context of the 1930s, the debate was set up solely in terms of the distribution of housing subsidy, and the confusion has continued to affect council housing for the last 60 years. After the Second World War rebating went into decline for a decade and so it was not until 25 years after the 1930 Act that governments began to encourage authorities to develop rent rebate schemes.

From 1955 until 1972 this took the form of urging authorities to redistribute their general housing subsidy in the shape of income related rebates. It was not until the Housing Finance Act 1972 that a specific rent rebate subsidy was introduced, but this still left local housing authorities with partial responsibility for a form of social security, and there then emerged the so-called 'better-off problem'. Many tenants were entitled to either a rent rebate or supplementary benefit, but it was sometimes difficult to tell which was the right choice.

The introduction of housing benefit in 1982/83 went some way towards eliminating that problem, and it represented a further major rationalisation in the sense that housing benefit was at last recognised as a form of social security, and responsibility for it in central government was transferred from the DoE to the DHSS (now DSS). Unfortunately, this logic was not applied at the local level and local authorities remained responsible for housing benefit administration.

The latest twist in the saga is that from April 1990, the so-called new regime for local authority housing finance once again blurred the distinction between housing subsidy and income maintenance. Provision for rent rebates was subsumed within the new housing revenue account subsidy, thereby raising again old arguments about better-off tenants subsidising their poorer neighbours — only this time local authorities had freedom to ignore central government policy.

Notes

1. *House of Commons Debates* Vol 230, col 973, July 1929.
2. Sir E Simon, *The anti-slum campaign*, Longmans, Green & Co, 1933, p.40.
3. M Stocks, *Eleanor Rathbone*, Gollancz, 1949, p.146.
4. Sir E Simon, *op.cit.,* p.24.
5. R Finnegan, 'Housing policy in Leeds between the wars', in J Melling (ed) *Housing, social policy and the state*, Croom Helm, 1981.
6. S Schifferes, 'Council tenants and housing policy in the 1930s', in *Housing and class in Britain*, Political Economy of Housing Workshop, 1976.

(This article was first published in ROOF in January 1990 and updated in December 1991).

Chapter 10

A prefab future

In the aftermath of the Second World War, housing shortages meant that bombers gave way to houses on the nation's production lines.

Martin Pawley

Because the appreciating house has for so long been the principal plank in the middle class black economy, it is difficult to remember what it was like when flats and houses were simply consumer goods like telephones or motor cars. Yet, only 40 years ago, that is what they were. Politicians, builders and householders all thought of housing as a product.

At the end of the Second World War the vast majority of people in Britain rented their houses, and expected to go on doing so all their lives. They rented them under terms of tenure that were actually less arduous than those enjoyed by the drivers of company cars today. It is interesting to remember this when people argue that ownership is a 'privileged' or 'democratic' form of tenure, while rental is 'oppressive' or 'feudal'.

Today, when 68 per cent of households in the country are owner occupiers, more than half the new car registrations are 'feudal' corporate perks. And the same people who would consider themselves to be in a state of 'feudal' servitude if they had not bought their own home, would also consider it 'oppressive' to have to buy their own car.

There is no good reason why all houses should appreciate like antique furniture. They could be as plentiful as cardboard boxes: they could be produced and sold like cars. The drivers of the shiny new Cavaliers and Sierras that roar off the forecourts each year do not own them: they 'rent' them on terms as oppressive as those endured by the frank-tenementers and free-socagers of medieval times, and yet they consider themselves a privileged motoring class.

This is a paradox that illuminates the way in which the consideration of any alternative to the sale and resale of expensive handmade houses has disappeared from the political agenda in recent years. Crowded out by massive mortgage-peddling, alternatives have only now, in the crisis of growing homelessness, begun to stir again.

The idea of mass-producing houses to conquer the problems of homelessness and overcrowding dates from the aftermath of the First World War, but prefabrication has a much longer history, stretching back long before Henry Ford began mass producing cars in 1913. William the Conqueror's army brought prefabricated forts to England in 1066, and transportable barracks and hospitals were shipped to the Crimea in 1854.

In the aftermath of the First World War 74 years later, nearly 30,000 steel and concrete prefabricated houses were built in Britain because of the housing shortage and the scarcity of skilled building labour. But these houses were not intended as short-life, replaceable units. As the Swiss architect Le Corbusier wrote in 1923: 'Most ordinary people equate getting a house with writing their will', and this misconception was to dog the prefabrication of houses right up till recent times.

Everywhere, except in the United States, interwar experiments in prefabrication took the form of heavy concrete or steel structures. Inevitably there were problems of cracking, leaking and corrosion and, because of the political and economic turbulence of the era, these problems were never solved by continuous technical development. In fact, the same prefabrication methods were to re-appear — along with the same problems — in the 1960s when heavy concrete system building enjoyed its last boom.

True mass production of houses began in America, the first country to motorise, and the first to become hypnotised by the promise of the production line. There, the average cost of a house had increased by 200 per cent between 1913 and 1926, while the average cost of a car fell by 50 per cent. Several individuals grasped the implications of this.

The first glimpse of a truly mass produced prefabricated home came in 1927 when Richard Buckminster Fuller, an inventor who had served in the US Navy during the Great War, patented a mast-supported prefabricated light alloy house that was air-deliverable — by airship. But Fuller was never able to put this house into production.

More conventional-looking production line dwellings were first onto the market. With the advent of the New Deal in 1933, special task forces like the Tennessee Valley Authority and the Farm Security Administration financed the development of light, timber-frame truckable dwellings that were produced in large numbers.

But the real boom in lightweight, short-life prefabrication came with the entry of the United States into the Second World War, when the needs of war production led to the rehousing of more than nine million workers and their families in less than three years. During this time, architects like Walter Gropius and Konrad Wachsmann, and inventors like Fuller, exploited lightness and expendability in successful mass production.

Post-war plans for making good the United States housing deficit involved the emergence of a massive prefabrication industry based on automotive and aviation technology. Bombers were to give way to houses on the production lines and aviation engineers planned their entry into the housing market.

During the war, British fact-finding teams went to the United States to study the creation of the new war-production towns by prefabrication. By 1944 in Britain, it was clear that the loss of 750,000 houses from bombing, the effects of rent control upon private landlords, four years of non-building and the imminent demobilisation of six million conscripted servicemen had created a massive post-war housing crisis that would erupt the moment the war ended. Successive wartime government committees considered the crisis, and their reports concluded that a state housing programme was the only answer.

This was a bipartisan conclusion. Modest building society proposals for a housing association-administered programme of private rental housing were rejected in favour of 'new

technology'. Just as in America Curtiss Wright aircraft engineers
were ready to plough their redundancy pay into 'housing
factories', so in Britain was the government paying for the
design of prefabricated houses to be assembled on the
production lines that manufactured Spitfires, Lancasters and
military trucks.

It was Winston Churchill, the Tory prime minister of the
wartime coalition government, who first announced the
Emergency Factory-Made or EFM housing programme. In
March 1944, he announced a Ministry of Works emergency
project to build 500,000 'new technology' prefabricated
temporary houses directly the war ended. 'The emergency
programme is to be treated as a military evolution handled by
the government with private industry harnessed in its service',
said Churchill. 'As much thought will go into the prefabricated
housing programme as went into the invasion of Africa.'

In the event, military planning provided less successful in
dealing with post-war economics than it had in dealing with the
enemy. The design of the Ministry of Works temporary houses
owed its origins to a number of wartime studies carried out by
the motor and aircraft industries. The first prototype to be
unveiled was the motor industry contribution, a steel panelled
'experimental temporary bungalow' called the 'Portal' after the
minister of works, Lord Portal.

With a floor area of 616 square feet — one third larger than
the minimum size laid down by the 1919 Tudor Walters report
on space standards in public housing — and an estimated cost
of £675 fully furnished, including fitted bathroom, kitchen and
refrigerator, the proposed rent for the 'Portal' was to be 10
shillings (50p) a week for a life of 10 years.

The next house was the 'Arcon', an asbestos-clad variant of
the 'Portal', with the same prefabricated kitchen and bathroom
capsule. Then came the most sophisticated of an eventual total
of no less than 1,400 proposed designs. The 'AIROH' house
(Aircraft Industries Research Organisation on Housing) was a
675 square foot, 10-tonne all-aluminium bungalow assembled
from four sections, each to be delivered to the site on a lorry,
fully furnished right down to the curtains. The four house
sections were linked, using the same type of bolted connection
as aircraft wing root joints. The proposed rate of production of

complete houses was to be an incredible one every 12 minutes. This was possible because the completely equipped and furnished 'AIROH' could be assembled from only 2,000 components, while the aircraft it would replace on the production line required 20,000.

In retrospect, it is clear that the EFM programme was the nucleus of what might have developed into a 'new technology' housing industry. Plans were made to use surplus airfield construction plant for site preparation, and records were set for speed of erection before the war ended. In April 1945, an 'Arcon' house was completed and handed over to its new occupants by 22 men in under eight hours. In May an 'AIROH' was erected on a bombed site in London's Oxford Street in just four hours.

But the EFM programme was not without its enemies. Even before the end of the war, the second reading of the Housing (Temporary Accommodation) Bill, which moved the allocation of £150 million for the production of prefabs, was refused by members who, like many people outside parliament, had come to believe that the 'Portal', the 'Arcon' and the 'AIROH' were intended to be the permanent houses of the future.

How far the alarm of the construction industry and the banks and building societies contributed to this myth has never been determined, but the state-funded construction of half a million prefabricated dwellings to be assembled by non-construction industry labour and let at controlled rents cannot have been a matter of indifference to the organisations that had dominated the housing market for so long. The establishment of a successful prefabricated housing industry based on automotive and aviation technology would have transformed, perhaps for ever, the balance that had historically existed between the scarce stock of existing housing and the rate of new construction.

In the United States, where the prefabrication boom of the war years left a well-established mobile home industry behind it, annual prefabricated short-life housing completions rose from 37,000 in 1946 to over 500,000 by the early 1970s. The existence of such an alternative source of housing in Britain would certainly, and repeatedly, have eased the problem of the homeless ever since.

In March 1945, the Coalition government published a white paper on housing policy, in which the first two years after the war were designated 'emergency production years'. During this time the EFMs were to play a vital part, with the first 150,000 allocated to local authorities to meet emergency housing need. By this time, rising labour and material costs, as well as some refinement of their design had increased the projected cost of all the EFMs, notably the 'Portal', which had been re-engineered so that it sat flat on the ground instead of being raised some six inches above it.

This meant that the unit cost for all EFMs had risen to between £800 and £1,400 — between 10 and 30 per cent more than the cost of a conventional house. The programme remained intact because of its promised speed, but its future was now precarious.

Clement Attlee's Labour party, which won the general election of July 1945 with a large majority, inherited the EFM programme when it took office and presided over the last act in the drama. Another housing white paper, published in August, confessed that the 'Portal' had been abandoned for lack of steel and announced yet more cost increases for the 'Arcon' and 'AIROH'. Nonetheless the new minister of health (then responsible for housing) announced in October 1945 that the programme would proceed together with conventional house construction and an aggressive policy of municipalisation for privately rented stock. By 1946, the ministry was issuing six housing directives a week. But in the event, the EFM programme contributed little to the total of 1.2 million new homes built between 1945 and 1950.

Production of the major types of EFM for local authorities continued until 1947, but only 170,000 of the 500,000 units Winston Churchill had spoken of were completed before the dollar convertibility crisis put a stop to the programme altogether. Of these, the largest number (54,000) were 'AIROH' houses, and 46,000 were 'Arcon'. The rest were made up of smaller numbers of different designs.

By chance one of the AIROH houses went to the mother and father of Neil Kinnock. In 1986 he remembered: 'It had a fitted fridge, a kitchen table that folded into the wall and a bathroom.

Family and friends came visiting to view the wonders. It seemed like living in a spaceship'.

The end of the prefab programme has a curiously modern ring to it, involving the value of sterling, overseas debts and the balance of payments. Notwithstanding Labour's concentration on domestic issues after the economically ruinous adventure of the war, it was evident by 1946 that an increased share of the nation's output of goods would have to be diverted into exports so that the international balance of payments could be restored.

Lend-lease, the wartime arrangement under which the United States had supplied Britain with food and raw materials in return for the allocation of greater resources to the war effort, had ended abruptly with the defeat of Japan and had to be replaced by a hastily negotiated £937 million loan, to be repaid over 50 years starting in 1950.

In the summer of 1947, the government allowed the exchange rate against the dollar (pegged at $4.80 since before the war) to float. Within five weeks, the Treasury lost 84 per cent of its dollar reserves. The British gross domestic product, worth 16 times the $2.4 billion reserve held in the spring of 1947, proved

Labour election poster 1945: a 'quick fix' was needed for Britain's post-war housing shortage.

inadequate to sustain sterling. Convertibility was abruptly ended but the crisis showed clearly that the allocation of 60 per cent of the country's resources to house building — which absorbed labour and contributed nothing to exports — was no longer possible.

From 1947 until the 31 per cent devaluation of 1949, everything had to be thrown into an export drive. In the end all the ambitious housing plans of the wartime coalition government, like those of the post-war Labour government, failed, because in the ultimate analysis, housing was just not important enough.

(This article was first published in ROOF in July 1989).

Chapter 11

DIY for the homeless

Squatting has a long history, from 17th century occupations, through post-war seizing of empty army camps, to the pitched battles of the 1960s.

Ron Bailey

With the thoughts and words of Gerrard Winstanley for inspiration, the first squatters occupied and cultivated waste lands in England in 1649:

> The sin of property we do disdain
> No-one has any right to buy and sell the earth for private gain
> From the men of property the orders came
> They sent the hired men and troopers to wipe out the Diggers' claim
> Tear down their cottages, burn down their corn
> They were dispersed but the vision lingers on.

And that vision — of homes (if not land) and freedom for all — does linger on, over 300 years later. The current squatting 'movement', although probably having less high ideals than its precursors of 1649, has achieved one thing that its ancestors did not: survival. It is over 20 years since the first tentative squat in an east London luxury block in December 1968, and over 20 years since the bloody battles of June 1969 when 'hired men' employed by Redbridge borough council tried to 'wipe out the [squatters'] claim' — and failed.

In 1919, soldiers returning from the front found few 'homes fit for heroes' and so, to the astonishment and rage of the government, they seized the empty homes to live in. Nearly 30 years later, a much larger outbreak of squatting occurred, starting in the spring of 1945 in Blantyre, Scotland. In the summer of that year the 'vigilante' movement, consisting largely of homeless ex-servicemen, was installing homeless people in empty properties in many areas, including Southend-on-Sea, Brighton and Hastings.

In May 1946, James Fielding and his family occupied a disused service camp in Scunthorpe, Lincolnshire, and this event sparked off further such occupations. A Squatters Protection Society was born, and soon hundreds of empty camps all over Britain were occupied. There were nearly 45,000 squatters by October 1946.

The movement spread to London and empty flats and hotels were occupied. There were massive street demonstrations. The culmination came in September when an attempt to occupy the Duchess of Bedford Buildings was thwarted by the authorities. Six communist organisers were tried and convicted.

Although this did succeed in stopping the movement in London, four points need to be made as comment. Firstly, it did not stop squatting throughout the country. Secondly, this was enormously successful — some 850 empty camps were actually handed over to the squatters by the Ministry of Works. Thirdly, although that particular event was communist-organised, the movement as a whole was certainly not (indeed the party had been cool towards the movement for some time and had even denounced the 'vigilante' groups of a year earlier). And fourthly, it is perhaps significant that it was only the more centrally organised operations that the authorities succeeded against.

In August 1965, Mrs Joan Daniels and her children were occupying 'homeless family accommodation' at King Hill hostel provided by Kent county council. They had been there for three months and were due to be evicted onto the streets in accordance with the 'three month' rule. Her children would then be taken into care as they had no home. Joan and her husband Stan, however, were not prepared to allow this. When the 'welfare' officials arrived to 'carry out their duty' they not only found Joan unwilling to go, but also that Stan had moved in (another breach of the rules — no husbands were allowed in this homeless family accommodation) and they had barricaded themselves in. The officials retreated, promising to return.

Other husbands moved in. More families defied the three month rule. The Friends of King Hill Hostel was formed. The battle lasted a year before Kent county council was forced to cave in and permit husbands and wives to live together, end the three month rule and the taking of children into care, and improve conditions at the hostel.

During that year all the might of the state had been used to try to crush the protest; injunctions were taken out against husbands visiting their families — when they defied the ban they were jailed for contempt of court.

But the council lost, despite being united in its attempts to crush this action: Labour councillors joined Conservatives in jailing the homeless. The only exception was the Conservative member for Ramsgate, Kenneth Joseph, who supported the campaign.

The campaign, and publicity given to the jailings, forced the councils to back down; 23 local authorities changed their 'no husbands' rule overnight. More protests followed — in Birmingham, at Abridge hostel in Essex and in Wandsworth. Abridge hostel (a dormitory — two rows of beds, no husbands — 'the worst shit hole this side of hell') was closed down after families and supporters moved in with carpenters to partition off the hostel and make separate compartments so that husbands could move in. At first the council tried to crush this, too. But it retreated — scared of another 'King Hill'.

I remember the phone call that Sunday in 1966 with Walter Boyce, the Essex social services director. We were in the hostel and the police had ringed the building. Mr Boyce was adamant. 'Alright, Mr Boyce,' I said, 'we've just finished at King Hill and we're quite ready for the same here . . .'

'You're the King Hill people?' interrupted Mr Boyce. 'Yes'. A long silence followed. Three days later the council announced the closure of the hostel and the rehousing of the families.

During these struggles, the idea of squatting had been aired by the homeless families themselves, along the lines of: 'If we don't get out of this place we should take over that row of empty houses down the road'.

And we did. First, a token squat on 1 December 1968; a second 24-hour stay on 21 December in an empty vicarage. And finally 'the big one' — 'the crunch'. The installation of families into empty houses — with the intention of staying. Houses in Ilford (Redbridge) were chosen. Council-owned; empty for years; due to remain so for another five or more.

We planned everything to the last detail: barricades; furniture; split-second timing; rope ladders; three months supply of food; camping stoves. We did not know what would happen and we prepared for every eventuality — including the law.

We had researched the law in minute detail and produced a 'legal warning' informing the authorities that they would be breaking the law (Statute of Forcible Entry 1381) if they evicted us without a court order. I had discovered this law after being charged with it (unsuccessfully) as a result of the occupation of the Greek Embassy. Many months' research went into this legal warning — and it worked. After some initial skirmishes, the police kept out of things.

The council thus had to seek redress in the courts — which they did. But unsuccessfully. We deployed a series of legal manoeuvres and won or evaded all legal attempts to remove us from the houses. For six months during 1969, the struggle was fought with more families joining the squat and the council behaving more outrageously to try to stop it (and, yes, just like Kent and King Hill, the Conservative and Labour groups united in trying to crush the homeless).

For instance, the council sent in workmen to smash up houses by sawing through joists, ripping out ceilings and stripping all the services. These were places in good condition, with up to ten years of life before redevelopment.

At 6am on 21 April 1969, Barrie Quartermaine, a so-called 'private detective', and his hired thugs appeared on the scene. Their calling card was a crowbar through the front door of the squatters' homes. They then charged up to their bedroom, dragged the squatters out of bed (children and all) and threw their possessions out of the window. When David Jenkins protested they smashed his jaw: he spent six weeks with it wired up. A reign of terror ensued. We were followed on the streets:

Olive Mercer, who was pregnant, was chased and smashed in the stomach with an iron bar. She miscarried.

We regrouped, re-occupied and even started to repair houses vandalised by the council. The authorities replied with criminal prosecutions: charging us with entering houses and committing unlawful damage. I submitted to the court that we had entered and committed unlawful repairs. We were acquitted.

So the 'hired men' were called in again — in larger numbers. At 5.30am on 25 June 1969 they arrived. We watched them gather in the street outside. They collected piles of rocks and bricks and bottles from neighbouring houses and at a signal from Quartermaine they attacked. Missiles were hurled at the house and came in through the windows. Luckily we wore helmets and these protected us. Meanwhile, other 'hired men' charged the door with a battering ram and swung grappling irons to erect ladders to try to get in through the windows.

They got in through the door — but we had loosened the floorboards and they fell down into the cellar. So they started

Southwark's 'first squatter family', the O'Connors, move into an empty council house in 1969 after being given notice to quit their privately rented bedsit nearby.

a fire to try to burn us out but we doused it with water and
tarpaulin. At this point, after 15 minutes of battle, the police
stepped in. Inspector David Millam stopped the fighting as he
'feared a breach of the peace was about to take place'!

We had won. I have preached and practised total non-
violence for all my political career *as a principle*, but I cannot
see what else we could have done that day. The families were
housed and Redbridge entered into negotiations for a short-life
housing deal with a local self-help group which we set up.

But it was outside Redbridge that the real effects of this
victory were shown. We installed families in empty houses in
Lewisham and the council wanted no Redbridge-style repeat.
It offered a deal: the squatters could have all the council's empty
houses if we agreed to vacate when the time came for
redevelopment. The council also agreed to 'point' squatters on
their pre-squatting (and therefore worse) accommodation.

The Lewisham Family Squatting Association was born. It is
still going. Interestingly, this first deal with a self-help group
was signed by a Conservative council. The Labour minority
accused the Tories of 'selling out to the anarchists' and called
for a battle.

Soon 'legal squatting', or what is now known as 'short-life
arrangements', was spreading to properties owned by the
Conservative-controlled GLC, Lambeth, Greenwich, Ealing,
Camden, Islington and Tower Hamlets. The Communist party,
which had supported the Redbridge struggle against 'the
reactionary Tory council', voted with the Labour majority in
Tower Hamlets in trying to crush the squatters, as we were
'splitting the working class movement'.

We had to outwit Southwark with legal delaying tactics and
publicity. Every statement we made was reasonable. We
'wanted to help the council solve its problems by using houses
they had no use for'; we offered to 'do up empty houses for the
council's homeless families'. Even when we bit hard it was 'so
bloody reasonable', as one councillor complained. Thus we
'asked the national Labour party to help' — by occupying
Transport House three days before the local government
elections. This 'ultra-reasonable' tactic was, and remains, an
effective way in which small groups can defeat powerful
authorities.

Gradually Southwark started to behave stupidly — smashing up empty houses, distorting figures and literally lying (we had leaked documents to prove it). We set up a 'respectable' front of 'heavyweights' to offer the council a way off the hook — a deal with Southwark Self Help Housing. What it did not know was that we controlled Southwark Self Help Housing.

The 'legal squatting' deals were working. The Conservative minister of housing, Julian Amery, recommended in 1974 that local authorities made arrangements with short-life groups and 'reliable squatters' organisations'. Thus was the current short-life property movement born.

We probably had four aims when we started back in 1968:

● sparking off a mass 'direct action for homes' movement

● achieving better housing by direct action

● radicalising attitudes to housing

● building a radical alternative housing force.

There is now a mass movement, although it took longer to develop than we hoped. There are probably between 20,000 and 30,000 people squatting and this figure has been fairly constant for the past ten years. For many people, squatting is the only answer to homelessness. Whereas 20 years ago no-one would have thought of squatting, now it is one of the answers. This can only be called a political consciousness.

I believe that virtually every improvement in national policy towards the homeless has been achieved by direct action. The authorities have been dragged along squealing; enlightened politicians backed the campaigns readily, and thereby assisted. But the strength and the initiative came because of successful and uncontrolled (and uncontrollable) direct action which has incurred the wrath and opposition of *all* the political parties.

(This article was first published in ROOF, May 1989).

Chapter 12

Building for the masses

Council housing played a major part in post-war
building programmes. How did it move from being
the subject of political consensus to the target for
spending cuts it has now become?

John English

Chapter 7 deals with the introduction of state subsidies for
council housing in 1919, and the development of the tenure
during the inter-war years. By 1939, council housing was
established as an important form of provision, accounting for
about ten per cent of the total stock. After 1945, successive
governments promoted the building of council housing, though
with varying degrees of enthusiasm, and the sector expanded
every year until the 1980s. But the housing policies of the
Thatcher government meant that a combination of right to buy
sales and a low level of new building resulted in its contraction.
Council housing has declined from a peak of about 30 per cent
of the stock in the 1970s, to little more than 20 per cent at the
beginning of the 1990s.

Governments of all parties supported the building of council
homes, both before and after 1945, for a variety of reasons.
Views about the proper role of council housing have varied
between the parties and over time. Sometimes it has been as a
safety net for the poor and to rehouse people from slum
clearance schemes; sometimes as a short-term expedient to get

Hulton Deutsch

Council houses in the shadow of Austin's factory at Longbridge, Birmingham, 1957.

houses built quickly; sometimes as the 'normal' working class tenure; and, briefly, as a potentially dominant tenure catering for all classes.

Political debates on the appropriate function of council housing can help us to understand how it reached its present state, and to put current arguments over the right to buy and 'residualisation' into an historical context.

The housing situation in 1945 resembled that in 1918; although the housing stock had been greatly expanded during the inter-war years, there had been virtually no building for six years, and bomb damage meant severe shortages. There was agreement between the parties that council housing would play a major role in the post-war building programme. The Tories also envisaged a substantial role for private enterprise, to which subsidies would be extended, but Labour wanted local authorities to dominate. Labour won the 1945 election, and proceeded to implement its programme under the leadership of the new minister of health, Aneurin Bevan.

As well as Labour's general pro-public sector ideology, there was a rhetoric of social mixing and rejection of 'one-class' council estates. The statutory restriction of council housing to the 'working classes' was repealed in 1949.

In 1945-51, over four-fifths of the houses completed were for public authorities (mainly local authorities). In 1951, the proportion was running at almost 90 per cent.

At Bevan's insistence, the new council houses were built to high standards, particularly of space. During this period, council housing came as close as it has ever come to being a 'universal' service like the NHS, potentially catering for practically the whole population. But in reality, Bevan's vision for council housing for all never came near to being achieved. Few non-manual worker-headed households have ever been council tenants. In any case, there was already too much owner occupation — amounting to about a third of the stock — to make it likely that council housing would ever be accepted as a 'universal' service.

The first effect of the Conservative election victory in 1951, when Harold Macmillan was appointed minister of housing, was that the output of council housing increased. It was not that the Tories became enthusiastic about general needs council housing, but the leadership had been bounced into a commitment to building 300,000 houses a year by the 1950 party conference after criticism of Labour's 'inadequate' record.

The basic Tory position was endorsement of owner occupation — a 'property owning democracy' — with council housing in a special needs role. But building for owner occupation could not be cranked up to a high level, so until 1953/54, local authority output was increased to unprecedented levels. Subsidies were raised, and Macmillan told local authorities to build as many houses as possible.

One way in which Macmillan was able to increase the output of council houses was by reducing space standards (a process started by the Labour government), to economise on bricks and timber. The so-called 'people's house' tends to be criticised as a retrograde step, but these houses have generally been popular and plenty have been bought under the right to buy.

The 1953 White Paper, *Houses: The Next Step*, made the government's position clear. 'One object of future housing policy will be to continue to promote, by all possible means, the building of new houses for owner occupation . . . While anxious to encourage the spread of house ownership, Her Majesty's Government have been equally conscious of the need for houses to meet the requirements of the greater part — perhaps necessarily the greater part — of the population. They have been careful to secure that the building of more houses to sell shall not prejudice the building of houses to let . . . This dual policy . . . will be continued'.

In 1954, Duncan Sandys replaced Harold Macmillan at the ministry of housing and once the overall target had been achieved in 1954, local authority output was reduced to below 300,000 for the rest of the decade (on the basis of what the economy could afford).

Private sector completions exceeded those in the public sector in 1958 and, with the exception of a brief period in the late 1960s, have remained in the majority. By the early 1960s, public sector output had settled down to around 40 per cent of the total.

Slum clearance, suspended in 1939, was restarted in 1954/55 and from then on, a substantial proportion of new council houses were used for rehousing. In addition, there was concern about the housing conditions of elderly people, many of whom lived in the private sector, and local authorities were urged to cater for them. The 1956 Housing Subsidies Act withdrew new subsidies for general needs building and limited them to dwellings for rehousing and one-bedroomed units. (The Act also notoriously encouraged high rise building by providing subsidies which increased with storey height).

The last few years of Tory rule up to 1964 were marked by a revival of council building from its low point around 1960. Housing was still a major political issue, and a great deal of argument centred on the rate of slum clearance.

The 1960s were also the era of system-built blocks of flats which were widely seen both as a way of boosting output where skilled labour was in short supply and of rehousing people from slums without undue resort to overspill. No doubt this was all done with the best of (somewhat paternalistic) intentions — it certainly was not a cheap policy — but it has burdened council housing with an appalling legacy of unpopular and difficult-to-let accommodation with which local authorities are currently struggling.

When Labour took office under Harold Wilson, the 'numbers game' was still rampant in housing politics and Labour announced a target of 500,000 houses a year by 1970 (this was never achieved and was abandoned with public expenditure cuts in 1967). Its 1965 White Paper called for a 'proper balance' between owner occupation and council housing. The building programme was to be split equally between the two tenures, implying some increase in the relative importance of the public sector but higher output in both. There were to be more generous subsidies for the public sector (introduced in the 1967 Housing Act).

'But once the country has overcome its huge social problem of slumdom and obsolescence . . . the programme of subsidised housing should decrease. The expansion of the public sector programme now proposed [is] to meet exceptional needs . . . The expansion of building for owner occupation on the other hand is normal; it reflects long-term social advance.' Labour endorsed owner occupation as the 'normal' tenure and saw the large-scale building of council housing as an essentially short-term expedient to meet 'exceptional' needs.

The 1965 White Paper also reiterated support for the disastrous use of novel construction methods — 'House building must be increasingly industrialised to get the numbers we need.' Parker Morris standards were to be mandatory for public sector building, providing for better space standards, space heating and so on.

In opposition, the Conservatives had moved towards a more vigorous policy of promoting owner occupation. Few council houses had been sold before the mid-1960s, but in 1967 and 1968 many urban local authorities were won by the Tories and some (notably Birmingham and the Greater London Council) started enthusiastically to sell council houses.

The Labour government did not oppose sales in principle, but argued that they were inappropriate in areas with high housing need, and so limited sales in many areas. In 1970 the new Conservative government removed these restrictions to encourage council house sales (though, despite backbench prompting, a right to buy was not introduced).

Sales increased but even in the peak year, 1973, they amounted to only about a third of public sector completions.

New building fell back to below the previous low point in 1961, though the public sector continued to expand throughout the period.

The other strand of Conservative policy was the 'reform' of public sector housing subsidies. These were a mess, having been built up over half a century and bearing no relationship to the financial position of particular local authorities. But subsidy reform was used as an opportunity to force up the level of council rents. Better-off tenants would pay more, thus reducing public expenditure, while no doubt encouraging them to consider owner occupation. At the same time poorer tenants — those who really should be council tenants — would be 'protected' by the new national rent rebate scheme.

Rent increases under the 1972 Housing Finance Act were halted by Labour in 1974. Much the same mix of policies, however — council house sales, higher rents and increased reliance on rebates — was to be used a good deal more effectively by the next Tory government after 1979.

The 1974 Labour government abandoned 'fair' rents in the public sector and existing subsidies were frozen pending the completion of a Housing Finance (later Policy) Review, which resulted in the famous Green Paper of 1977. Council housing seemed to be doing well for a brief period: the owner occupied market moved from boom to slump, there was an increased demand for council housing, and speculative builders were glad to sell completed estates to local authorities.

But the bubble burst by 1976/77: new council building, which had been increased, fell away again under the impact of public expenditure cuts.

The 1977 Green Paper reiterated successive governments' support for owner occupation. A right to buy (promised by the Conservative opposition) was rejected and rent increases were to be in line with average earnings, but the comments on tenure were not drastically different from the position of the Tory government after 1979. 'An increasing number of people want to own their own home. The Government welcome this trend . . . For most people owning one's home is a basic and natural desire, which for more and more people is becoming attainable.' The Green Paper recognised that 'one of the consequences of the continuing growth and wider access to home-ownership could be gradually to narrow the social make-up of the public rented sector.'

In fact, the residualisation of council housing was already well under way. The Labour Cabinet apparently considered adopting the right to buy and so stealing a popular Tory policy.

The right to buy was initially controversial. Some councils tried to delay its implementation, and for a time Labour promised to repeal it. But within a few years it was accepted by all parties and it has become a permanent feature of British housing. Over one and a half million public sector (mainly council) houses have been sold, and the public sector fell from just under a third of the housing stock in 1979 to little more than a fifth in 1991.

The 1980 Housing Act was largely a rerun of an abortive bill introduced by Labour shortly before they lost office, with the addition of the right to buy. Both included new rights for public sector tenants such as security of tenure. Exchequer subsidy was to be reduced on the basis of government assumptions about annual rent increases — local authorities had little alternative but to raise rents.

By the mid-1980s, the government had succeeded in its immediate objectives. But a great many council houses remained which were not going to be purchased by individual tenants. The future of rented housing was reviewed, and the 1987 White Paper, *Housing: The Government's Proposals*, proposed that housing subsidies were to be 'reformed' again and housing revenue accounts 'ring-fenced'.

The government's long-term aim was that local authorities should ideally cease to be landlords, transferring their stock to housing associations, and should be confined to a 'strategic' or 'enabling' role. These proposals were incorporated in the 1988 Housing Act.

As owner occupation has grown, it has attracted large numbers of working class households which were once the backbone of council housing. Council housing has increasingly become the tenure of non-working households dependent on social security benefits. These processes have been summed up as the 'residualisation' of council housing. It is impossible to say that residualisation began at a particular time, though it was underway in the 1970s if not before.

It is sometimes said that council housing is becoming, to use an American term, 'welfare housing'. Public rented housing as a whole in Britain is still very different from the tiny and highly stigmatised public sector in the United States, although the similarities are greater in the case of some difficult-to-let estates. Nevertheless, successive governments have rejected changes to housing subsidies and taxation which might have permitted the public sector to provide an attractive alternative to owner occupation for those able to exercise choice.

Residualisation has now gone much further and will undoubtedly continue. Council housing has lost its positive image and much of its political constituency: getting a council house may be a lifeline for the homeless, single parents and others without choice, but most people do have choice and few of them consider the public sector.

The extent of further residualisation will depend largely on how far owner occupation can grow: the scope for this may be fairly limited in England and Wales though there is clearly potential for continued expansion in Scotland. The substantial growth of home ownership, at least south of the border, must depend to a considerable extent on whether low income owner occupiers are given more financial assistance. The problem of mortgage default at the beginning of the 1990s was partly a result of increasing numbers of economically marginal households taking on the commitments of house purchase. Housing benefit could, for example, be extended to mortgagors at relatively modest cost (see Steven Webb and Steve Wilcox, *Time for mortgage benefits*, Joseph Rowntree Foundation, 1991).

There is also scope for mortgage lenders to provide 'packaged' arrangements covering maintenance, insurance and so on. Care and Repair schemes have done something on a very small scale for the elderly. It is perhaps surprising that a government which is so pro-owner occupation has not done more for the poorer home-owner.

A substantial public sector is likely to remain for a long time. The tasks of housing departments were once mainly routine, such as the collection of rents and organisation of repairs. Now there is a major element of individual care and supervision which requires different skills from staff. Many management tasks, for the frail elderly, the mentally ill, or disabled people, are really an aspect of care in the community. Other tasks relate to coping with the limited personal and social competence of many younger tenants.

The role of council housing has constantly evolved over the years. A large public sector may be seen as an essentially transitional phase in housing provision which was required when the private rented sector was in decline but the extension of owner occupation to the bulk of the population did not seem feasible.

Mistakes have been made, but overall, council housing has made a major contribution to improving housing conditions in Britain. One thing that is certain is that the role of council housing will continue to evolve.

(This article was first published in ROOF in November 1991 and updated in January 1992).

Chapter 13

An unwelcome home

Far from being welcomed with open arms, post-war migrants from the West Indies and Asia faced discrimination and racism in every housing sector.

Susan Smith & Sara Hill

In 1948, Britain passed a Nationality Act. It was the price paid for creating Commonwealth from Empire, and it entitled the people of the ex-colonies to British citizenship. The right to live and work in Britain, protected by the law and insured by the welfare state, was part of this package. So, of course, was an obligation to pay tax and to live within the law.

But the story since 1948 has been one of political compromise: it is a story of extracting obligations while curtailing entitlements. The social history of housing — the negotiable right to shelter — provides a sobering illustration.

After the Second World War, Britain, like so many other European countries, had an urgent need for cheap labour. Traditionally, we are told that the government recruited West Indian (and later south Asian) migrants, and welcomed them with open arms.

Cabinet papers tell a different tale. The government did everything it could to recruit migrant workers from anywhere *but* the New Commonwealth. It preferred European workers: displaced people from Germany, Austria and Italy, East European refugees, and anyone else who the Royal Commission

on Population (reporting in 1949) could be sure 'were of good
human stock and not prevented by their religion or race from
intermarrying with the host population and becoming merged
with it.'

The preference was for migrants who were not citizens, and
had no right of abode or entitlement to welfare. The
government wanted workers who would not compound the
'threat' of ghettos becoming established in the port areas, and
who would be more 'fitted' than 'colonial peoples' to the kinds
of jobs available.

In the end, the demands of the economy won, and colonial
immigration was encouraged. But scarcely had the invitation
been issued than the Cabinet turned its attention to future
immigration controls. Throughout the 1950s, administrative
arrangements discriminated against black immigrants. Strict
proof of British nationality was demanded, shipping lists were
tampered with to put migrant workers at the back of the queue,
passports were delayed, and travel certificates were often faulty.

With this ambivalence towards black citizens, it is easier to
understand (though not to justify) why no attempt was made
in those early years to co-ordinate immigration with housing
policy. Migration to Britain was initially seen as numerically
limited, short-lived and, crucially, temporary. As MP Harold
Davies put it, when discussing the role of 'colonial' workers:
'Having helped our productivity and output, that manpower
or womanpower could go back to the Colonies and be a nucleus
of productivity there'. (Hansard 1946-47, vol.441, col.1415).

It was never expected that the migrants would stay, and
governments did not encourage them to do so by providing
accommodation. Employers received no incentive to find
homes for their workers (in contrast to the pattern in several
other European countries).

Politicians would not formally entertain the possibility that the
'white' British public, or the institutions in which they worked,
might discriminate against black households. Britain was, after
all, a world leader in tolerance and understanding: racism was
a problem for foreign, not domestic policy. Thus, despite the
efforts of Fenner Brockway and a few Labour party colleagues
(who annually introduced a Bill to outlaw discrimination from
1956), the 1950s and much of the 1960s passed with no serious

Hulton Deutsch

Black man looking for accommodation, 1958: notices like 'no coloureds' were legal until 1968.

concern for the difficulties black (Afro-Caribbean and Asian) people had in finding accommodation. There was no legal protection for those denied a home because of the colour of their skin. Yet, throughout this period, homes *were* denied on 'racial' grounds in every sector of the housing system.

The private rented sector was often the migrants' first port of call. By the late 1940s, it was already a residual sector for the white population. Properties were often old, in poor repair, reserved for multiple occupation and located in the inner city.

Private renting was often the only option for Afro-Caribbean and, later, Asian migrants. But this was by no means an open sector. The exclusionary banner: 'No blacks, no Irish, no dogs' was quite legal until 1968, and even in that year, the clause 'no coloureds' was included in more than a quarter of adverts for rented accommodation placed in a local newspaper circulating in London's East End (*Guardian*, 2.8.68).

Stories like that of Tony Overman, who rented a double room in a boarding house but was asked to leave because his wife was black (*Daily Herald* 1.1.54), abound in the press cuttings of the 1950s.

Even in 1964, over half the rented properties in Oxford were unavailable to African or Asian students (*Guardian* 26.11.64) and in 1965, the Milner Holland Report indicated that only a third of private landlords in London would let their dwellings to 'coloured' tenants.

It has been suggested that, as a consequence of discrimination, a split market occurred in private renting. Black people were effectively restricted to properties owned by black landlords, and this pushed up rents and encouraged overcrowding. For this, and other reasons, black tenants in the private sector have always had accommodation of lower than average quality, in which they must live at higher than average densities, for greater than average rents.

As the 1950s unfolded, public housing became a cornerstone of the welfare state and it promised a solution to the post-war housing shortage. Local authorities were required to allocate homes according to need, rather than ability to pay. By virtue of their low incomes and housing needs (especially when joined by their families), New Commonwealth migrants should have been eligible for council homes. However, in the procedures adopted to determine housing need, it was soon apparent that white people's needs were to be ranked above those of their black counterparts.

Even by the mid-1960s, only six per cent of the overseas-born black population had secured access to council housing, compared with 28 per cent of Irish migrants and about one third of the rest of the population. Something was preventing black people from getting council housing. This something was the reluctance of local politicians and white communities to allow black citizens the same welfare benefits as their white counterparts.

The early 1960s saw a rash of colour bar petitions submitted to councillors by white council tenants. The example of the Loughborough Road Estate in Brixton is reported in the *Daily Mail* (28.9.64). Five hundred tenants complained about the allocation of a two-bedroomed maisonette to a black family. Their spokesperson is quoted as saying: 'There are many British families who need a home without it being given to immigrants. We have a nice housing estate here and that's how we want it to stay'.

The same sentiments were expressed by the occupants of Bank Street Flats, Wolverhampton, who threatened to leave *en masse* when they discovered a flat was to be let to a black family (*Daily Express* 6.6.66).

This notion that the citizenship rights of 'coloured' immigrants did not extend to living in council housing was more often reinforced than resisted by the councils themselves. (Though it is important to recognise that in recent years, many local authorities have spearheaded the anti-racist housing movement.) In 1965, the Smethwick housing management committee is reported to have recommended that a new 15-storey block of flats should not be made available to black families because 'when people find coloured people moving in they become apprehensive' (Committee chairman, cited in *The Times* 6.5.66).

In 1966, the Birmingham borough Labour conference openly rejected a proposal to allocate council houses on new estates to black applicants.

Apart from this overt policy of exclusion, housing departments often imposed access rules which effectively prevented black families from queuing for a council home on equal terms with white applicants. The most notorious of these were residence requirements, which meant that people had to live in the area for a number of years before being allowed onto council waiting lists. This obviously excluded recent immigrants, and today, such requirements are recognised in law as indirect discrimination.

Residence requirements were 'justified' in a variety of ways. As the chair of Wolverhampton's housing committee put it in

1967: 'It seems reasonable to us that if someone comes to this country, they should wait two years. They may not like it here and may go back' (*The Times* 8.9.67).

In Birmingham, a five year residence requirement was retained until 1977, and it has been suggested by some researchers that demand from local whites was systematically exaggerated to keep this rule in place, to limit the number of black applicants admitted to the housing lists.

In the mid-1960s, white households were 26 times more likely than their black counterparts to have secured a council home. This was hardly a reflection of differences in housing need, but local politicians preferred a happy electorate to an open housing system. Patricia Hornsby-Smith MP observed that: 'If the housing committees allocated their property exclusively on the basis of social need, no white family would get anywhere near an allocation for the next ten or 15 years.' (Hansard 1971, vol.813, col.118).

Such exclusion needed a response. A vigorous black housing association movement was established, and it flourished towards the end of the 1950s. This succeeded for some years in filling at least part of the housing gap for black people. Some of these associations later catered to a wider public, but many closed or were taken over by large 'white' associations following the Housing Association Act 1974. It is only more recently that the Housing Corporation has recognised the importance of black-led initiatives and is working with black people to rekindle the black housing association movement.

Excluded from the public sector, discriminated against in the private rented sector, many Asian and (to a lesser extent) Afro-Caribbean households turned to home-ownership. Here they faced discrimination in applying for mortgages, and their choice of homes was further limited by the activities of estate agents, as well as by resistance from existing white owners.

In the absence of legislation against discrimination, the Bradford Equitable Building Society was able, in 1957, to explain in writing to a 37-year-old Jamaican civil servant and LSE graduate that: 'It is the policy of the society's directors not to approve advances to coloured people' (*Sunday Pictorial* 21.7.57). Other societies may not have been so open, but research shows that conventional mortgage finance was (and sometimes still is) denied to black people on the grounds of who they are and where they live.

In the 1960s it was possible for estate agents to respond to the demands of groups like the Southall residents' association, which, in 1963, claimed that 'the problems these immigrants are introducing are numerous and too apparent' and wrote to estate agents asking them to 'restrain your activities with regard to coloured people' (*The Times* 9.11.63).

It was also possible, and legal, for a Wolverhampton property developer to ban the sale of 300 new houses to 'coloured' families (*Guardian* 12.8.65). And it was possible for the Rowley Regis residents' association in Staffordshire to ask to buy the home of a local Jamaican family on the grounds that 'we do not want coloured people on our estate. We do not want the value of our property to diminish' (Chairman of Rowley Regis residents' association, cited in the *Daily Mail* 31.5.65).

As a consequence of low incomes and discrimination, black people found cheap homes in the inner and middle rings of the major cities, usually in areas scheduled for clearance or blighted by short leases. Their dependence on 'unconventional' loans (often over short periods with high repayments and high interest rates) excluded them from the tax concessions associated with home ownership. Their homes were often costly to maintain and repair, yet research shows that they made relatively limited capital gains through several periods of house price inflation.

Politicians knew the difficulties facing black Britons during the 1950s and early 1960s. The Attlee Cabinet considered the problems of discrimination in employment and housing. In 1955, a Conservative Cabinet also acknowledged that: 'The most serious problem arising at present from coloured immigration is undoubtedly in the field of housing'. But the response was not to legislate against discrimination, or to intervene in other ways. Politicians responded instead by introducing immigration controls which infringed the entitlements of black Britons even more.

Politicians had always feared the development of 'racial' segregation. It suggested colour bars and civil unrest. But by the late 1950s, the segregation of black people, socially and geographically, into some of Britain's worst housing, had already happened. In Parliament though, segregation, poor housing, unemployment, overcrowding and deprivation were depicted simply as the consequence of having too many 'coloured colonials' packed into too little space. This, it was argued, was an environmental hazard, a drain on resources, and a threat to the urban landscape. As a problem of numbers and location, the 'solution' seemed obvious.

This solution, claimed the Conservatives after their annual conference in 1961, was to restrict immigration. The benefits would include the integration and dispersal of those already settled, and it would help solve the housing problem as well. It was also a vote winner, appealing to the 'common sense' of a public still gripped by the moral panic whipped up from the 1958 Notting Hill riots. And controls would help Britain's entry to the EEC, since they would protect European housing and labour markets from any future influx of Commonwealth migrants.

The 1962 Commonwealth Immigration Act was not passed because it made economic sense, and the Labour party opposed the Act on grounds of economic irrationality. The Act was passed because it proposed to solve a crisis of 'race relations' which was emerging in the inner cities. As Rab Butler, then Conservative home secretary, put it: 'The greater the numbers coming into the country, the larger will these communities become and the more difficult it will be to integrate them into our national life . . . there is a real risk that the drive for improved conditions will be defeated by the sheer weight of numbers' (Hansard 1961, vol.649, cols.694-5). So the right of abode, guaranteed in 1948, was restricted in 1962. Britain failed (on that occasion) to enter the EEC, but the policies of 'race' generally had moved to centre stage.

Matters came to a head in the October 1964 general election. Harold Wilson spoke out on *Panorama* against the slogan allegedly adopted by Conservative candidate, Peter Griffiths. Griffiths was said to be fighting for Smethwick on the platform: 'If you want a nigger [for your] neighbour, vote Labour,' and in a surprise victory, he snatched the seat from Labour's Gordon Walker. The racist vote had become an electoral advantage. There was no incentive for politicians to press for a more open system.

In 1968, Enoch Powell, publicly lamented 'the transformation of whole areas . . . into alien territory' (Birmingham speech, 20 April 1968). In that same year, the Labour party relinquished its unpopular opposition to immigration control, and moved swiftly to limit the entry of Asians fleeing persecution in Kenya. An uneasy consensus had been achieved.

Labour justified its 'U turn' by introducing two Race Relations Acts, in 1965 and 1968. These were to act with immigration restrictions to promote integration (which was still thought to hinge on dispersal).

But these Acts were too little, and too late. The marginal housing position of black people had already been established, and the 1965 Act neglected to address discrimination in housing and employment in any case! The second Act remedied this, but indirect discrimination was not outlawed until 1976. No attempt was made to co-ordinate this legislation with housing and urban policy, and for at least ten years, achievements were limited.

The seeds of entrenched racial inequalities in housing — inequalities which exist even today (sometimes in a different form, and sometimes via different mechanisms) — were sown over 40 years ago. They were sown through politicians' dogged insistence that racism was alien to the British character, by their obsession with the idea that anti-discrimination laws were tantamount to a colour bar, and by an ill-founded (but politically convenient) assumption that early patterns of segregation — and the housing problems embedded in them — could best be solved by immigration controls. The rights given to black Britons in 1948 were never fully exercised and have been compromised by a tendency to manage the housing and legal systems with an eye to political expediency rather than social justice.

(This article was first published in ROOF, March 1991).

Chapter 14

The ghost of Rachman

Policies on the private rented sector have varied over the past 30 years, but the decline continues.

Peter Kemp

Ever since the first Rent Act was passed in 1915, landlords have had more or less strict controls imposed on their ability to increase rents or evict their tenants. Over the same period, renting from private landlords has decreased dramatically, down from 90 per cent in 1914, to 32 per cent in 1960, to only about seven per cent today.

Once the mainstream tenure, private renting is now on the margins of housing provision. Decline has mostly been in the unfurnished subsector: furnished renting has stayed at around two per cent of the total housing stock in recent years (see Table 1). Most new lettings are now furnished, a part of the market that was outside of rent control until 1974.

The decline of private renting has been the result of a complex set of processes, including rent control. But the co-existence of long term decline and different forms of rent regulation has led many to see the latter as *the* cause of the former. This belief, combined with a preference for markets and a dislike of regulation, lay behind the Conservative's 1988 Housing Act.

During the debates on the 1987 Housing Bill, many commentators referred to the 1957 Rent Act, the last time that a major rent deregulation was introduced. A last ditch attempt

Table 1

PERCENTAGE OF HOUSEHOLDS IN BRITAIN RENTING UNFURNISHED OR FURNISHED PRIVATE HOUSING

	Unfurnished	Furnished	Total
1971	12	3	15
1975	10	3	13
1979	8	2	10
1983	5	2	7
1987	4	2	6
1988	4	2	6
1989	4	2	6

Source: General Household Survey.

to revive private investment in rented housing, it was one of the most controversial measures passed by the Macmillan government. As Barry Cullingworth has pointed out, the parliamentary debates during the passage of the 1957 Rent Act had a curious air of unreality about them. Very little was then known about private landlords, and both parties relied on caricatures and oversimplified analyses.

For the Tories, rent control was the cause of the decline of private renting. Remove rent controls, they argued, and rents would increase (but not *too* much, since the post-war housing shortage had eased by then). Higher rents would mean larger profits for landlords and, therefore, an increase in the supply of private lettings. It was all as simple as an elementary lesson in basic economics. Left to itself, the private market would produce the goods: the supply of, and demand for, rented houses would reach an equilibrium, and both landlords and tenants would benefit; the one from higher profits, the other from an increased supply of houses to rent.

Labour, in contrast, portrayed the 1957 Rent Act as a 'vicious' piece of class legislation that would profit landlords, but cause serious hardships for tenants, without increasing the supply of rented homes. Rent controls were a necessary safeguard against the all-too-common tendency of private landlords to charge exorbitant rents and exploit their tenants, especially in the face of the housing shortage which still existed in areas like inner London. For many Labour MPs, the decline of private renting was inevitable, even desirable. The answer was not decontrol, but municipalisation of the remaining stock and an expansion of council house building, the subsidies for which had been cut back in 1956.

The 1957 Rent Act had three main measures. First, all of the more expensive houses were decontrolled at once. This applied to all dwellings with a rateable value of over £40 in London and £30 elsewhere. Second, less expensive houses became decontrolled when the sitting tenant left, a procedure known in the trade as 'creeping decontrol'. And third, the maximum rent that a landlord could charge on property that remained in control was raised to more or less twice the rateable value.

The Act's impact was, generally speaking, much less dramatic than either of these alternative scenarios predicted. The Rowntree Housing Study, led by Professor David Donnison, found that many landlords *did* put up their rents (some by a considerable amount), but others did not. Decontrol did not produce an increase in investment in rented housing. Rather, disinvestment continued and, indeed, it seems the rate of decline increased, rather than decreased (see Table 2). The average decline in the 62 months up to June 1956 was 236,000 dwellings a year. Between 1956 and 1961, the privately rented sector declined from more than a third to only a quarter of the total stock of dwellings.

Table 2
ESTIMATED NUMBER OF PRIVATELY RENTED DWELLINGS, GREAT BRITAIN, 1951-1961

Date	No. of dwellings	% of total
April 1951	6.2m	45
June 1956	5.4m	36
December 1961	4.1m	25

Source: Report of the Committee on the Rent Acts, 1971, p.80.

Decontrol provided many landlords with the opportunity to get out of the sector by selling to owner occupiers, including their own sitting tenants. At the same time, most of the dwellings demolished in slum clearance schemes were owned by private landlords.

It was not until the early 1960s that many of the darker consequences of decontrol became apparent, partly because some of its provisions were postponed until 1961. By then, the housing shortage in places like inner London had become quite severe, especially at the bottom end of the market. With controlled rents well below market levels, creeping decontrol meant that landlords had an incentive to remove their sitting tenants by whatever means they could, in order to charge a higher rent. In the late 1950s and early 1960s, stories began to appear in the local press about intimidation of tenants, evictions and homelessness.

What transformed the situation, however, was the storm of publicity surrounding the west London landlord Peter Rachman. His nefarious activities came to light in the wake of the Profumo scandal in 1963. It turned out that one of the call girls involved in the Profumo 'sex and security' scandal had earlier been Rachman's mistress. The addition of slum landlordism to the already potent media cocktail of sex and national security allowed the press to inject new life into the Profumo affair. The fact that Rachman was dead by then conveniently removed fears of libel writs that might otherwise have restrained the media. For a couple of weeks, the public was fed a daily dose of stories about the violence and intimidation Rachman was said to have used against his tenants.

Sorting out the myths from the facts about Rachman may not be easy, but some things are clear. Born in Poland in 1919, he came to England in 1946. According to the Milner Holland Report, he first became a landlord in 1954, having acquired four houses in Shepherds Bush. Gradually, he built up a portfolio of rented houses (the precise number is not known), mostly in the Notting Hill area in west London. Many of these properties were in poor condition, but because of the shortage of rented houses he was able, once he had got rid of the sitting tenants, to let them at very high rents. Many of his tenants were alleged to be prostitutes.

By the late 1950s, Rachman was being investigated by the police for dealing in prostitution, by the Inland Revenue for tax evasion, and by public health officials about the state of his properties. The ownership of his properties was held by over 20 companies between which he continually transferred them. Evading the authorities became increasingly difficult, and by 1961 Rachman had disposed of almost all of his rented houses. He died in 1962, leaving £72,830 before tax.

Labour made considerable political capital out of the episode, and the ailing Macmillan government was forced to set up the Milner Holland Committee to investigate London's housing problems. The committee's report, published in 1965, concluded that there was an acute shortage of rented housing in London. The surveys commissioned by the committee found that although most tenants were satisfied with the way their landlords treated them, landlord abuse was too common to be dismissed as an isolated problem. The 1964 Labour government attributed its electoral success in part to housing, and passed a new Rent Act in 1965. This established the system of regulated tenancies and 'fair rents' assessed by independent rent officers that the Conservative's 1988 Housing Act abolished on new lettings.

The ghost of Rachman still haunts the Conservatives. Despite their commitment to deregulation, it was not until they had been re-elected for a third term of office in 1987 that they felt able to introduce decontrol of private lettings. And even then, as they were at great pains to stress during the debates on the Housing Bill, it applied only to *new* tenancies: the rights of sitting tenants were largely unaffected. Indeed, the Conservatives strengthened tenant protection against harassment in order to allay fears about a return of Rachmanism.

Rachman has come to symbolise the unacceptable face of private landlordism in Britain. He has given the English language a new word — Rachmanism — to describe the conduct of landlords who charge exorbitant rents for slum housing. For today's opponents of decontrol, Rachman is used to illustrate the adverse results of decontrolling rents.

So deeply engrained is the unsavoury image attached to landlordism that respectable private institutions have been wary

Popperfoto

Peter Rachman, the London property owner who made a fortune as a slum landlord and whose name became linked to the Profumo scandal in 1963, after his death.

of investing in houses to let, quite apart from the fact that while one government may decontrol rents, another may just as easily reintroduce controls. During the 1980s, successive Conservative ministers at Marsham Street set about trying to rehabilitate the private landlord's image.

In 1980, Michael Heseltine introduced the 'assured tenancy' scheme by which approved bodies (but not individuals) could let new (and later, reconditioned) properties at market rents. When he was secretary of state, Nicholas Ridley talked about the need to 'exorcise the ghost of Rachman'. And in 1986 John Patten, then housing minister, talked of creating a new breed of 'model' landlords. 'This isn't people with alsatian dogs trying to kick down the door and evict you', he told ROOF in 1987. 'After all, who could possibly object to renting from the Halifax or the Woolwich?'

But, even though approved organisations like the Prudential were able to build new properties for letting at market rents under the assured tenancy scheme, very few did so. By April, 1987, only 742 old-style assured tenancies were constructed for letting (the more widely quoted figure of 2,993 assured tenancies included dwellings built for shared-ownership and a large number of units on 99 year leases built by MacCarthy and Stone).

This lack of a supply-side response to the deregulation of new and refurbished property was partly due to the shady image attached to private landlordism in Britain (though not overseas). It was also because removing rent controls was only a necessary, but not a sufficient, condition for a revival of private renting. The main factor now inhibiting a return of investment in privately rented housing is, quite simply, the limited effective demand for this type of accommodation.

As well as decontrolling new lettings, the 1988 Housing Act abolished the 'approved landlord' scheme. New lettings now have to be either new-style assured tenancies in which tenants have the right to remain if they pay the market rent, or assured shorthold tenancies which are also let at market rents but for defined periods of time (with a minimum of six months) after which the landlord can regain possession. Organisations like NACAB and SHAC have suggested that many landlords are choosing to let on shortholds because of the guaranteed right of repossession, in preference to assured tenancies.

Whether the changes made by the 1988 Housing Act will indeed revive the privately rented sector, it is still too early to say. As in 1957, there is once again considerable divergence of opinion as to what will be the effect of this latest deregulation.

The government argued that deregulation would help recreate a 'commercially viable climate' for private renting. By allowing artificially restrained rents to rise to market levels, it would increase the supply of private lettings and thereby widen tenant choice. Critics of deregulation, on the other hand, pointed to an entirely different outcome. They argued that, far from heralding a revival of private renting, it would instead mean a return of Rachmanism. Deregulation of new lettings, said the critics, would give landlords an incentive to evict their sitting tenants so that they can create new-style assured tenancies at market rents.

In fact, the outcome of deregulation is unlikely to be as dramatic as the rhetoric of either the critics or the advocates of this policy have suggested. This is mainly because it was wrongly assumed that most lettings prior to the 1988 Act had a rent registered with the rent officer. According to a representative survey carried out in 1982-84, 90 per cent of *new* lettings — the market affected by deregulation — didn't have a registered rent. A more recent survey found that, in 1988, three-quarters of all private lettings in England didn't have a registered rent (see Table 3).

Table 3

PRIVATE RENTED SUBSECTORS IN ENGLAND: 1988 and 1990

	1988 (%)	1990 (%)
Regulated with registered rent	26	18
Regulated without registered rent	33	15
Resident landlord	6	4
Not accessible to general public	28	27
(rented)	(13)	(13)
(rent free)	(15)	(14)
No security	4	5
Shorthold or assured	4	30
Total	100	100
(000s)	(1,741)	(1,698)

Source: OPCS, 'The 1990 private renters survey: preliminary results', OPCS Monitor, SS91/2, 1990, p.3.

In effect, therefore, the official deregulation embodied in the 1988 Act formalised something that had already largely occurred. While assured and shorthold tenancies give the tenant significantly less protection than regulated tenancies, they are more secure than licence agreements. Prior to deregulation, there was considerable uncertainty about whether a letting was a licence or a tenancy in law.

In order for the supply of privately rented housing to increase significantly, thus reversing decades of decline, rents will have to rise substantially. The question is, has deregulation paved the way for a big rise in rents? This is not easy to answer, not least because registered rents were (and still are) rising anyway and, in the present inflationary environment, unregistered rents would probably have risen too. The position has been further complicated by the slump in the owner occupied housing market. Thus identifying the impact of deregulation *per se* is not straightforward.

Yet since 90 per cent of new tenancies were already at market rents, it is unlikely that deregulation, by itself, will stimulate a sufficiently large increase in rents to induce much new supply. Moreover, rent to income ratios were already very high in the private sector before the 1988 Act came into force (see Table 4). In 1988, over half of all private tenants were paying more than 20 per cent of their total net income on rent and rates. A third were paying more than 33 per cent. Of the tenants most likely to be affected by the 1988 Act, around half were paying more than 33 per cent of their net income and between two thirds and three quarters were paying more than 20 per cent. The scope for significant rent increases in the private sector, therefore, is unlikely to be great.

Although a general increase in rents could occur if housing benefit were increased to pay for it, the odds are against it. In 1988, about a quarter of all private tenants were in receipt of housing benefit. These payments have been cut back several times over the past few years, and they may well be cut again if the total cost increases substantially.

Moreover, rent officers now have the role of policing housing benefit claims by private tenants. Between 1 April and 31 December 1989, over a quarter of rent officer determinations held that the rent was too expensive or the accommodation too large. Given the low incomes of people on housing benefit and the already very high average rent-to-income ratios, tenants affected by these determinations will not find it easy to make up the difference between the rent assessed for benefit purposes and the rent that the landlord is actually charging.

The rent officer referral procedure therefore seems to be a restraining influence on rents, though one which may cause tenants real hardship. Although the government decontrolled new private lettings, for those tenants on housing benefit it, in effect, re-introduced a form of regulation through the back door.

Table 4

PERCENTAGE OF ALL PRIVATE TENANTS IN 1988 WHOSE RENT PLUS RATES WAS MORE THAN:

	A third of net income	A fifth of net income
All tenancies	34	54
Regulated with registered rent	46	76
Regulated without registered rent	38	66
Resident landlord	44	66
Not accessible to general public	22	27
No security	50	75
Limited security	55	74

Source: T Dodd, *Private Renting in 1988*, HMSO, 1990, p.50.

But even if the decontrol provisions of the 1988 Act are unlikely significantly to reverse the decline of private renting, has it provided unscrupulous landlords with an extra incentive to harass and evict the substantial number of sitting tenants who do still have a registered rent? The answer appears to be 'probably not'. Landlords already had an incentive to get rid of their sitting tenants with registered rents, either to relet outside the Rent Acts or to sell to the owner occupied sector. In this sense, Rachmanism has not returned, because it never really went away.

The GLC's 1983-84 survey of private tenants in London, for example, found that about one in 20 had suffered harassment from their landlord in the previous year. In the 1988 private renters survey, four per cent of tenants in London and two per cent elsewhere in England said their landlord had tried to evict them, while six per cent in London and two per cent elsewhere said that their landlord had offered them cash to leave. On the other hand, 80 per cent of all private tenants felt they were on good terms with their landlord and only three per cent were on bad terms (the remainder were on neither good nor bad terms).

Thus, in a relatively small but significant number of cases, harassment was already a serious problem before the 1988 Act.

Early results from a recent OPCS private renters survey suggest that regulated tenancies have declined from 59 per cent of lettings in England in 1988 to only 33 per cent in 1990, while shorthold and assured tenancies have increased from four to 30 per cent of lettings (see Table 3). This marked change has largely been a function of the rapid turnover — most of it voluntary on the part of tenants — that exists in the furnished sub-sector of the market.

The OPCS private renters survey found that the number of private lettings fell by 43,000 between 1988 and 1990, representing a decline from nine to eight per cent of the total housing stock in England. But it also found that the number of lettings started in the two years prior to the 1990 survey was 49,000 more than were started in the same period prior to the 1988 survey.

Although it would be easy to attribute this apparent increase in the number of recent lettings to deregulation, there are two reasons for exercising caution before accepting this explanation. First, because of the slump in the owner occupied housing market, some owners unable to sell their homes have let them out until the housing market picks up once again. This may therefore produce only a short-lived boom in the supply of private housing to let. Second, the slowdown in the rate of decline of private renting actually began several years *before* deregulation came into effect. The decline of the sector may simply have bottomed out even without deregulation.

In fact, it is too early to tell whether deregulation has helped to reverse 75 years of decline in the privately rented sector. All that is clear at this stage is that any change in the sector is likely to take place only gradually.

Decontrol of private lettings is therefore unlikely to produce the dramatic results that either the critics or the advocates of the policy suggest. It will neither solve the problems, nor make things much worse. If the 1957 Rent Act did not revive private renting, neither will the 1988 Act do so *by itself*. But it would be a mistake to assume that history will simply repeat itself, for circumstances today are very different from 1957. Then, almost all unfurnished private lettings had a controlled rent at well below market levels. Hence 'creeping decontrol' gave landlords a real incentive to get rid of their tenants. In 1988, most tenants did not have a registered rent but were already paying what the market would bear. Yet two important lessons for today can be drawn from the 1957 Rent Act saga.

First, deregulation is not enough to revive private renting. At the very least, it would also be necessary to reduce the fiscal privileges of home-ownership. Successive governments have so feathered the home-owner's nest with tax relief that anyone who can afford to buy generally does so. But most of the people who have to rent cannot afford to pay the level of rents that landlords require to make letting good quality housing a profitable business. Thus, unless the fiscal privileges of home-ownership are removed, or equivalent subsidies put into privately rented housing, this sector of the housing market is unlikely to revive on a significant scale.

The government is unwilling to abolish mortgage tax relief, but it did extend the Business Expansion Scheme to include rented housing on assured tenancies for a five year period. However, there are no plans to extend the BES, or find a more cost effective replacement, after 1993. It seems unwilling to recognise that deregulated rents, together with only a five year 'kickstart' to investment via the BES, is not enough to provide a commercially viable private rented sector. Without a reform of housing finance, a more long term tax incentive scheme is essential for private renting.

Second, an effective policy for private renting requires bi-partisan political support, not least because houses are an investment that outlive any one government. Labour has said it will consider some form of tax incentive for private landlords, and has begun to accept the need for a viable private rented sector, but while considerable progress has been made towards a more consensual approach to private renting — due largely to Labour's new found pragmatism — there is, unfortunately, still some way to go.

(This article was first published in ROOF, November 1990, and updated in December 1991. The original article was a revised and extended version of an article which first appeared in New Society).

Chapter 15

The road from Clay Cross

The refusal of Clay Cross councillors to implement the 1972 Housing Finance Act was a landmark in the battle to defend the principle of local autonomy in setting council rents.

Peter Malpass

On 1 April 1974, Clay Cross urban district council ceased to exist. In the nationwide reorganisation of local government, this small mining town became merely a constituent part of the new district of North East Derbyshire. But the events of the previous two years meant that the name of Clay Cross would survive as a symbol of local resistance to the power of central government.

The story of the Clay Cross councillors' refusal to implement the fair rent provision of the Conservative government's Housing Finance Act 1972 is a heroic saga of determination to defend the living standards of council tenants and the rights of duly elected representatives to decide policy for their locality. For a year after all other authorities had bowed to the apparently inevitable rent increases, the Labour-controlled Clay Cross council stood alone and continued its defiance, in spite of the measures taken against it by the government and the lack of support from the national leadership of the Labour Party.

The Housing Finance Act, and Clay Cross's part in its undoing, raised fundamental questions about the nature of local authority housing. More widely, the episode raised questions about circumstances in which citizens in a democracy can justifiably defy laws passed by Parliament.

In housing terms, the issues were about the level of council rents, the principle of means testing as the primary method of determining entitlement to subsidy, and the freedom of local councils to determine their own housing policy. Given that the government was determined to raise rents and to remove local autonomy in rent setting, both of which were widely opposed in the country at large, the issue then was: How could opposition be mobilised and made effective, and how far could local authorities reasonably pursue their opposition to the law?

These issues and the lessons of the early 1970s are of continuing relevance today in the context of the poll tax and another bout of centrally imposed council rent increases. Although the stand taken by Clay Cross in 1972-74 was important then, and remains relevant now, it is necessary to learn from the Housing Finance Act episode as a whole.

The story began with the election of a Conservative government in June 1970, and the appointment of Peter Walker as the first secretary of state at the newly formed Department of the Environment. Walker was an established advocate of the extension of 'fair rents' into the public sector, and in July 1971 he published a White Paper, *Fair Deal for Housing*, in which it was argued that housing problems in terms of slums, overcrowding, dilapidation and individual hardship, could only be cured by a radical reform of housing finance.

Then, as now, the owner occupied sector was regarded as untouchable, and the scope of radical reform was confined to the rented sectors.

The main objective was to establish a uniform system of fair rents for all public and private sector tenants. On the one hand, in the private sector the government wanted to hasten the replacement of very low controlled rents by much higher fair rents, with their built-in tendency to rise in line with inflation. On the other hand, it wanted to raise council rents from levels which were perceived by ministers to be kept unacceptably low by a combination of the politically motivated politics of Labour-controlled local councils and a subsidy system which distributed assistance in a very perverse way.

In this context, the government view was that fairness required all rents to be set in the same way, using the criteria for fair rents which had been introduced for the private sector by the Labour government in 1965. It therefore proposed an entirely new system of subsidies for council housing, in which Exchequer assistance would be related to the deficit on the housing revenue account, after income from fair rents had been set against expenditure on loan charges, repairs and maintenance.

It was quite clear that the transition to fair rents would lead to some very considerable rent increases around the country, and thus to a substantial saving in subsidy expenditure by central government. However, the savings were to be offset to some extent by the introduction of a mandatory scheme of rent rebates for low income council tenants (and a similar scheme, termed rent allowances, for private tenants). This was presented by ministers as a shift from indiscriminate subsidy of houses to a more targeted and fairer system of subsidising people.

In terms of pricing policy, fair rents represented an attempt to break away from historic costs as the basis for rent setting, and to substitute a system based on current value as determined by market forces of supply and demand. The opposition, however, described the proposals as a vicious attack on working class living standards and a crude attempt to cut public expenditure behind a smokescreen of rhetoric about fairness.

From the point of view of local councillors the scale of implied rent increases was matched in importance by the way in which the proposed system removed all local authority discretion to set rents in line with locally determined housing policy. For 50 years, local authorities had considerable autonomy to set council house rents (although in fact variations from place to place were more closely related to variations in scale and timing of new building than rents policies as such). Councils had also enjoyed complete freedom to decide whether to have a rent rebate scheme, and the form and generosity of any scheme.

Under the terms of the new system set out in the White Paper, authorities would have a duty to set provisional fair rents for all their dwellings, but the final decision would lie with a special independent committee for each area. The members of these committees would be drawn from the same panel of people who adjudicated on private sector fair rent cases.

Thus the long established tradition of local autonomy in rent fixing was undermined in two ways: first, by the requirement to adopt the contentious market-based, fair rent criteria, which many local councillors and supporters of council housing saw as completely inappropriate in the public sector; and second, by the denial to local authorities of the right to be the final arbiters of fair rents in their area. In future council rents would effectively be set by non-elected, non-accountable committees entirely separate from local authorities themselves.

The government's initial assumption was that fair rents would be substantially above existing rent levels, and it therefore required authorities to make a series of annual increases, equivalent to 50p per week, until fair rents were reached. In the early 1990s, a 50p rent increase may seem quite modest, but in 1972 it represented an increase of around 25 per cent for most tenants. It should also be remembered that the idea of a rent increase *every* year was not then as well established nor as widely accepted as it has since become.

It was not surprising, therefore, that councillors and tenants in Clay Cross and a great many other places were outraged by the prospect of substantial, compulsory, rent increases every year for the foreseeable future. The Labour party was strongly opposed to the principle of fair rents in the public sector, and from the second reading of the Housing Finance Bill in November 1971, Labour was committed to repealing the fair rents provisions affecting local authorities. In Parliament, the opposition fought the Bill by tabling no fewer than 581 amendments in the 57 sittings of the standing committee, but delaying tactics had only nuisance value and the government of course secured its legislation.

The real opposition had to take place outside Parliament, and in particular at the local level. In a move which paralleled the stance of the Labour leadership on the poll tax, the Labour party leaders in 1972 refused to support local authorites which defied the law and refused to implement the rent increases.

Without a clear lead from the parliamentary party, local authority opposition failed to coalesce into an effective force. Nevertheless, the Housing Finance Act brought the issue of council rents to a level of political prominence never previously achieved and the scale of the local opposition was impressive. A contemporary observer described it like this:

'Literally thousands of marches, demonstrations, pickets and meetings were held in which hundreds of thousands of people took part. Millions of leaflets were distributed all over the country and large numbers of organisations were set up to co-ordinate the opposition. Hundreds of Labour councillors, by initially refusing to implement the Act, laid themselves open to surcharges and disqualifications from public office. Even when all but a very few Labour councillors capitulated to one or other of the battery of central government threats, up to one hundred thousand local authority tenants continued to struggle against the Act by refusing at one time or another to pay the increase imposed under it.'[1]

At first, more than a hundred authorities declared their intention to ignore the Act, but one by one they changed their position, until in October 1972, when the first increases were due, fewer than 50 remained. None of the big urban authorities, apart from the London borough of Camden, carried its

The Clay Cross Rebel Eleven: Labour held all 11 seats on the council, due in part to its low rent policy.

opposition into 1973. Eventually there were only two authorities where the councillors adamantly refused to implement the Act.

One was the small South Wales authority of Bedwas and Machen, where the secretary of state for Wales used his power to install a commissioner to take over the housing duties of the local authority. Within three months of the Act taking effect, the commissioner was in position and continued to collect higher rents until 1974.

The other rebel authority was Clay Cross, which differed from most councils in that the Labour party held all 11 seats on the council.[2] This position of strength was largely based on the local party's housing policy, including a policy of low rents. Well before the Act took effect in October 1972, Clay Cross council had made clear its refusal to implement the rent increases; if the government wanted higher rents then the councillors took the view that the government would have to be seen to be carrying out its own policy, and this meant installing a housing commissioner.

However, the government's first action was to declare Clay Cross in default of its duties, and to give a deadline for compliance. This was followed in November 1972 by an extra-ordinary audit of the council's accounts, resulting in the councillors being personally surcharged and automatically debarred from their positions. The district auditor's decision was appealed to the High Court in London, where the appeal was lost, with costs awarded against the Clay Cross councillors. It was not until October 1973, a year after the Act came into force, that a commissioner was finally appointed to take over housing administration in the town.

The opposition did not end, however, and the authority refused to co-operate with the commissioner, forcing him to establish his office in nearby Chesterfield. It was the proud boast of the council that in six months, the commissioner failed to collect a single pound of extra rent from tenants in Clay Cross.

The 11 rebel councillors lost their last court battle in January 1974 and finally accepted disqualification from office. Elections were held, and ten of the 11 seats were won by supporters of the Labour rebels, but within two weeks the council was abolished by reorganisation.

It is tempting to see the Clay Cross story as an indication that strength and determination can win through even against the might and power of central government. It is also worth noting that the government was slow to act against Clay Cross, and never actually used all the powers at its disposal.

On the other hand, the fame of Clay Cross derives from the fact that it was the only authority in England to take a defiant position, and it is important to consider why other authorities failed to sustain their opposition to the Act. This must be related to the Labour party leadership's failure to support defiance of the law.

Local autonomy is all very well when it is the discretion of one's own supporters that is at stake, but from the point of view of Wilson, Callaghan and others, the concern was to avoid providing justification for Tory authorities refusing to implement Labour legislation in a future parliament.

It is clear that the civil service drew some lessons from its experience with Clay Cross. The Clay Cross councillors were given plenty of opportunities for *public* defiance, and for high profile media occasions (such as High Court appearances in London). All this sustained their campaign and made law enforcement clumsy and unseemly.

However, the Housing Act 1980 relied on *financial* mechanisms for raising rents, thereby denying opportunities for publicity or open defiance. The new regime for local authority housing finance introduced in 1990 uses exactly the same approach and will be just as hard to oppose.

Thus, although the Housing Finance Act was defeated by the return of the Labour government in 1974, new means have been devised to pursue its objectives of higher rents and less local autonomy. The struggle continues.

Notes

1. L Sklair, 'The struggle against the Housing Finance Act', in R Miliband and J Saville (eds) *The Socialist Register 1975*, Merlin Press, London 1975, pp.250-292.
2. D Skinner and J Langdon, *The story of Clay Cross*, Spokesman Books, Nottingham, 1974.

(This article was first published in ROOF, January 1989).

Chapter 16

A sense of duty

A private member's bill in 1977 was a turning point in securing a basic right for homeless people to be housed by local councils.

Janet Richards

The Housing (Homeless Persons) Act 1977 was a landmark in British housing policy. It placed the first ever duties on housing authorities to help homeless people and established homelessness as an integral part of the housing function.

Both the Poor Law and the National Assistance Act of 1948 treated homelessness as a welfare problem. Under the Poor Law, homeless people could get shelter in the workhouse, provided they had a right to settle in the district. Homeless people were typically regarded as undeserving and feckless, and workhouse conditions were harsh and punitive. The legacy of this regime had a lasting influence on attitudes towards homeless people, and policies to help them.

The National Assistance Act 1948 abolished the Poor Law and Section 21(1)(b) put a duty on county authorities to provide temporary accommodation for persons in urgent, or unforeseen need. Ministry of Health circular 87/48 stressed that the purpose was to assist people made homeless through an emergency such as fire or flood; it was not intended to deal with the 'inadequately housed'.

Welfare and social services departments which assumed the duty tended to interpret the Act as a hostel and casework service, with the result that deterrent Poor Law practices lived on. Conditions in temporary accommodation were usually inadequate and often in former Poor Law institutions. Communal facilities, sex segregation and time limits on stay were common.

Families were frequently split up. Some hostels would not permit men, and children were sometimes taken into care, leaving the parents to find their own accommodation. In 1974/75, 2,800 children in England and Wales ended up in care solely because of homelessness.

Many authorities applied eligibility criteria, for example by refusing to help pregnant women until after the birth. They also typically refused to accommodate people who had previously lived outside the area, which led to families being shuttled between authorities with neither accepting responsibility. Differences in local authority practices meant that geography played a large part in determining the chances of getting help.

The 1948 Act was incapable of coping with the scale and nature of post-war homelessness. The number of homeless people seeking help grew every year, and the majority were not victims of an emergency, but of the housing shortage. They needed permanent homes, which welfare departments, with no housing stock, were unable to provide.

Housing departments were usually unwilling to house homeless people, as they were seen as undeserving and irresponsible. To house the homeless was considered contrary to waiting list principles. Co-operation between welfare and housing departments was poor, and hindered by the fact that in most parts of the country they were in different tiers of local government.

The central weakness of the Act was that it treated homelessness as a welfare matter and gave duties to the ministry of health (later the DHSS) and social service authorities, when homelessness was a housing problem, with the ministry of housing and local government (later the DoE), and housing authorities, holding the key.

This split responsibility left a policy vacuum in which, for nearly 30 years, neither ministry took decisive action to change the legal framework. The ministry of health was even reluctant to use its default powers to enforce the law. The ministry of housing's *laissez-faire* approach to housing authorities precluded it from interfering in their rehousing policies. So homelessness was a subject 'on which government expressed concern, commissioned research, set up working parties and issued guidance and advisory circulars, but did not legislate'.[1] Moreover, any advice that was issued was largely ignored by local authorities.

For example, the Central Housing Advisory Committee's 1955 report *Unsatisfactory tenants* advocated that housing departments be responsible for housing homeless people, as did joint MOH/MHLG circular 4/59 and the 1968 Cullingworth report *Council housing, purposes, procedures and priorities*. The 1968 Seebohm Report on local authority personal social services recommended that homelessness duties be transferred to housing authorities. This conclusion was reiterated by the DHSS-commissioned Greve report (1971) on homelessness in London, and both this and research by Glastonbury (1971) for another DHSS inquiry clearly showed the 1948 Act to be ineffective.

Throughout the 1960s and early 1970s, the case for reform mounted. Academic research demonstrated that homelessness was primarily caused by housing shortage rather than by personal inadequacy. Voluntary groups and charities publicised the problem and there was growing public concern and media interest in the plight of homeless families, particularly after the screening of the television play 'Cathy Come Home' in November 1966.

Yet, despite evidence that the 1948 Act was not working and homelessness was in fact increasing, the Local Government Act 1972 reduced the duty to provide temporary accommodation to a discretionary power, with effect from April 1974.

This prompted Shelter, the Catholic Housing Aid Society, the Campaign for Homeless and Rootless, SHAC and the Child Poverty Action Group to form the Joint Charities Group (JCG) with the aim of seeking amendments to the 1974 Local Government Bill to restore the statutory duty and impose it on housing authorities. Although the amendments were unsuccessful, the campaign led to a DHSS directive, reinstating the duty, and secured an Opposition pledge that a Labour government would bring in laws imposing the duty. Over the

Shelter

Ten years after 'Cathy Come Home', Shelter campaigns with CHAS, SHAC and CPAG for homelessness duties to be imposed on local authorities.

next two and a half years, the JCG pressed for legislation to give housing authorities statutory responsibility for homelessness.

In February 1974, the Conservative government responded to the many reports calling for a duty on housing authorities with a joint DoE/Department of Health/Welsh Office circular 18/74, which took effect at the same time as local government reorganisation. This circular later proved significant in forming the blueprint for the Homeless Persons Bill and the Code of Guidance.

It acknowledged that homelessness was an 'extreme form of housing need' and recommended that housing authorities take over homelessness duties from social services. The circular also introduced the concept of priority groups. It advocated that where the housing situation was particularly difficult, authorities should give priority to families with dependent children and to single people made homeless through emergency, or vulnerable because of old age, disability, pregnancy or other special reasons.

There was now a clear anomaly in government policy: the statutory duty to assist the homeless lay with social services authorities, but government was advising housing authorities to take on the task.

A Labour government was returned in the general election of February 1974, but despite pre-election pledges, homelessness legislation was not among its priorities. The following year it initiated a review of homelessness, but its consultation document said that the government was not convinced that new legislation was appropriate.

A DoE survey into the implementation of circular 18/74, carried out for the review, revealed that by April 1975 most authorities had not adopted the priority group criteria and only a third of housing departments had accepted sole responsibility for the homeless. In some areas, neither housing nor social services would accept responsibility, with the result that families were shunted backwards and forwards.

By late October 1975, the government concluded that legislation was necessary after all. Homelessness was a growing political embarrassment. In 1976, around 33,700 households were accepted by authorities in England — more than double the number in 1971. Faced with pressure from all sides for legal reform, and with DoE research supporting this view, it was clear that circular 18/74 would only be implemented if it had the force of the law.

In Spring 1976 the DoE began separate, but parallel, consultation meetings with the local authority associations (LAAs) and the JCG to consider proposals for legislation. The JCG played an influential role in the consultation process, as DoE officials relied on its advice and support in resisting local government pressure for a limited duty.

The government's lack of commitment to the legislation became apparent when it dropped the Homeless Persons Bill from the 1976 Queen's Speech, ostensibly because of insufficient parliamentary time. However, it indicated that it would support a Private Member's Bill on the subject. Fortunately the Liberal housing spokesman, Stephen Ross MP, came fourth in the private members' ballot and agreed to adopt a Bill prepared by the JCG, but was permitted to use the DoE's own Bill, which was better drafted.

Although the Bill had government backing and sponsors from all parties, its prospects of becoming law were threatened by the government's slender majority, and it was at risk of not surviving the parliamentary session.

The Lib-Lab pact in Spring 1977 brought some relief on this front, and was instrumental in securing more parliamentary time for the Bill, but even so a safe passage was not assured, because it did not reach Standing Committee until mid-June and had to complete its stages by the end of July.

The objective of the Bill in its original form was to give legislative power to circular 18/74. It provided a statutory definition of homelessness and gave housing authorities duties to secure accommodation for people in priority need and to advise and assist others. The Bill reflected the JCG's position except that it also wanted a statutory right of appeal, default powers for the secretary of state, the extension of priority need to cover single people, and a requirement that the accommodation provided be reasonably suitable for the person's needs.

The Association of County Councils (ACC) was largely in favour of the provisions, but the Association of District Councils (ADC) and the Association of Metropolitan Authorities (AMA) were concerned about the cost of implementation and the loss of local autonomy. They did not want a legal definition of homelessness, or a statutory right to housing, but preferred a general duty on housing authorities to give homeless people advice and help to secure accommodation.

The ADC and the JCG emerged as the dominant opposing lobbies; the JCG briefed Stephen Ross while the ADC's case was fought by Conservative MP Hugh Rossi and fellow backbenchers.

The Bill's opponents argued that it would be unfair to applicants on the waiting list; would result in people deliberately making themselves homeless; would swamp authorities in desirable areas, such as seaside resorts, which, they claimed, would attract influxes of homeless people; and would restrict local discretion. They vilified the Bill in parliamentary debates as a charter for 'queue-jumpers', 'rent-dodgers', 'scroungers and scrimshankers.'

The opposition succeeded in weakening the Bill through amendments which said that people deemed intentionally homeless were not entitled to accommodation, limiting the authority's obligations only to people with a local connection, and defining priority need and vulnerability in vague terms.

These concessions were made to avoid delays that would have killed the Bill. The ADC and AMA counter campaign also carried weight, because its members would have the job of implementing the new law and their co-operation was vital if the Act was to work.

So the Act that came on to the statute books was a compromise measure. It was less liberal than circular 18/74, and legitimised the continuation of practices which limit help to local people, and discriminate between the 'deserving' and the 'undeserving'.

Nevertheless, it was an achievement in securing basic rights for homeless people, and was the first significant attempt by government to tell councils whom they should house. The JCG hoped that it would be the first step towards more comprehensive duties to all homeless people.

The legislation was later consolidated in the Housing Act 1985 and the Housing (Scotland) Act 1987, and in 1988 the main provisions were extended to Northern Ireland by the Housing (Northern Ireland) Order 1988 No 1990 (NI23).

The Act requires housing authorities to provide advice and assistance to homeless people and to secure accommodation for those in priority need, who are unintentionally homeless and have a local connection. Priority need is defined as pregnancy, having dependent children, being vulnerable because of old age, mental illness or handicap, or physical disability or other special reason, and being homeless or threatened with homelessness as a result of an emergency such as flood or fire.

Authorities are required to have regard to the accompanying Code of Guidance which gives advice on interpretation and good practice, but they are not obliged to follow it. The Code reflects the spirit of the original Bill in advocating a wider interpretation of the authority's duties than is laid down in the Act.

The number of households accepted as homeless under the Act has steadily risen: DoE figures record increases in England from 53,110 in 1978 to 145,800 in 1990. The law has primarily benefited families with children, who form the majority of acceptances and others in priority need, many of whom would not have received help in the past.

Since the Act came into effect, the two main reasons for acceptance as homeless have been the breakdown of sharing arrangements with relatives and friends, and breakdown of a relationship with a partner. The pattern has changed little, except that mortgage default has recently grown in significance, but it is different from pre-Act days when eviction by private landlords, and rent arrears, were major causes.

The Act has curtailed bad practices such as splitting families and taking children into care. The local connection rules and the LAAs Agreement on Procedures for Referral of the Homeless have reduced the incidence of inter-authority disputes over responsibility. And fears that the Act would lead to homeless people converging on popular areas have proved unfounded — DoE figures show that most households accepted as homeless were resident in the area one year previously.

However, the Act has certain gaps and flaws: the duty to secure accommodation does not extend to non-vulnerable single adults and young people, so it has done little to relieve the growing problem of homelessness among these groups. The definition of homelessness does not encompass homelessness resulting from violence from persons outside the home, or racial and sexual harassment. Applicants have no right of appeal, so can only challenge a decision through judicial review on grounds that the authority has acted contrary to the principles of administrative law, but such actions are costly and difficult to bring.

The Act's main failure is in not achieving uniform and consistent practice throughout the country. Authorities have considerable discretion as key terms such as 'intentionally homeless', 'vulnerable' and 'appropriate advice and assistance' are loosely defined.

With no statutory right of appeal, no default procedures and a Code of Guidance that has no statutory force, differences in interpretation and implementation have been inevitable, resulting in marked local variations in rates of acceptance and declaration of intentional homelessness.

For example, a DoE survey by Evans and Duncan (1986) found that having rent arrears and moving to an area to seek work were regarded as 'intentional homelessness' by 45 per cent and 55 per cent of authorities respectively, while 40 per cent of authorities did not accept children leaving care as homeless.

The Audit Commission's report *Housing the homeless: the local authority role* identified similar discrepancies in policy and procedures and highlighted the need to improve performance. But it also acknowledged that many homeless persons units operated under extreme pressure and that stress areas needed higher levels of investment in order to cope with demand.

The Act has never been backed with adequate resources for housing authorities, and has operated in a period of deepening housing crisis. It was introduced in a time of economic recession, rising unemployment and falling housing expenditure, all of which have since got worse. The decline of the private rented sector, the sale of council houses, and successive cuts in housing investment and new building have created a growing shortage of affordable housing, leaving councils to deal with increasing numbers of homeless people while having fewer properties in which to rehouse them.

As a result, homeless people accepted under the Act are getting a growing share of council lettings — in England the proportion increased from 14 per cent in 1978/79 to 30 per cent in 1989/90, and in London from 25 per cent to 59 per cent over the same period (DoE HIP figures). The proportion of family-sized homes let to the homeless is even higher, and the co-operation of housing associations in providing accommodation has become vital.

The notion that the homeless are 'queue-jumpers' has not gone away, but, as the Audit Commission study shows, most of the homeless are already on the waiting list.

The shortage of permanent lettings means that the Act has brought a growth in, rather than an end to, the use of temporary accommodation. In England some 55,300 households were in temporary accommodation in June 1991. The financial and social costs of such accommodation, and bed and breakfast in particular, continue to cause concern.

In 1988 the government initiated a review of homelessness legislation, prompting fears that the statutory duties would be dismantled. Both the voluntary sector and the local authority associations (with the exception of the ADC) urged that the law be left intact.

The government concluded that the law should remain unchanged, but decided to review the local connection rules in order 'to moderate undue demands on the most heavily burdened areas', and to review the Code of Guidance 'to help secure greater consistency between authorities.'

As yet, the LAAs have made little progress in reviewing their referrals agreement, mainly because only the ADC is in favour of change.

The New Scottish Code was published in May 1991, followed in August by the revised Code for England and Wales. They give guidance on good practice and, unlike previous Codes, they both emphasise the need for performance monitoring and suggest performance targets for processing homelessness applications. History shows that the Code is unlikely to be implemented comprehensively unless it has statutory force and authorities have the resources necessary to carry out its advice. Given their financial constraints, it is not surprising that many authorities do the minimum required by law rather than adopt the Code's more liberal approach.

Only by tackling the shortage of affordable housing will the prospects for homeless people improve. Until then, the safety net of the Act will increasingly be strained as councils find it ever harder to find permanent homes for homeless people.

Notes

1. N Raynsford 'The Housing (Homeless Persons) Act 1977' in N Deakin (ed), *Policy change in government*, RIPA 1986.

(This article was first published in ROOF, September 1991).

Chapter 17

The right to buy

Housing policy has been reshaped by the sale of one and a half million council homes since 1980.

Ray Forrest & Alan Murie

Selling council houses was the most substantial element in the privatisation policies of the Thatcher government, a privatisation which has benefited ordinary working families rather than the wealthy or those with capacity to shift their investment portfolios around. In the last 12 years some one and a half million public sector dwellings have been sold. Most of these sales have been under the right to buy introduced in the Housing Act 1980.

Those who have bought have mostly bought good houses at cheap (discounted) prices, and in general they have benefited from house price inflation. In some cases, they have bought because it is cheaper to buy than to rent. Rising interest rates have probably had less impact on those who bought under right to buy than on those who bought at market prices elsewhere. However the impact of recession and job losses is felt by this group as much as any other.

Evaluating council house sales over the last 12 years is complex. The policy has not operated in a vacuum. It has formed part of a general reshaping of housing policy.

The council sector has not only changed because of sales. It was already changing in important ways through the long established decline of private renting, the privileged treatment

---

THE CHANGING FACE OF COUNCIL HOUSING

- Fewer economically active
- Fewer multiple earner households
- Fewer higher income households
- Declining level of car ownership
- More households with no earners
- Declining role as family housing
- Increase in female headed households
- Increase in unskilled manual workers
- More elderly people
- Ageing dwelling stock
- Declining proportion of 3-4 bedroomed houses
- Increasing proportion of flats
- Increasing proportion of lettings to the homeless
- Increasing proportion of tenants on state benefits

---

of home ownership and social, economic and demographic change. There is no simple cause and effect between selling council houses and what has happened to the public sector. Most obviously, the effect of one and a half million council house sales would have been very different, had a major public sector building programme been taking place at the same time. It is important, therefore, to consider sales not just in terms of who has benefited and what has been sold, but in terms of the indirect and longer term changes which will flow from sales and in terms of their role in the broader policy context.

Selling council houses is not a new policy. Significant sales have been completed at various stages and legislation has consistently included powers for sale with ministerial consent. In the post-war period, refusals to countenance such sales gave way to a general consent to sales in 1951. There followed a period of fluctuating central government encouragement for sales, and different responses at a local level.

The Housing Act 1980 changed the formula. The power to sell with approval from the secretary of state continued, but for most council dwellings, a right to buy was also introduced.

This and subsequent legislation involved three key elements:
● council tenants were given a right to buy
● substantial discounts were given, linked to length of tenancy and applied to a market valuation
● council tenants were given a right to a mortgage from their local authority.

Through the 1980s, discounts were raised progressively to encourage further sales. By 1986, maximum discounts on houses stood at 60 per cent after 30 years' tenancy. Those in flats qualified for 70 per cent after 15 years. The original justification for discounting prices for council house sales (prior to the right to buy) derived from the lower value of properties in the private rented sector with sitting tenants as opposed to vacant possession. The link to length of tenancy came later, and the discount rate has become no more than a balancing act between providing sufficient incentive to maintain sales and generating a certain level of capital receipts. Substantial discounts and the right to buy have been backed up by a major publicity campaign and rising rents and, lately, changes of landlord have been partly designed to encourage purchase.

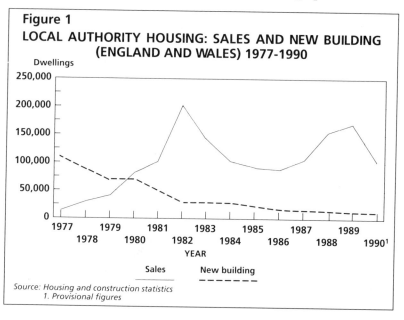

Figure 1

LOCAL AUTHORITY HOUSING: SALES AND NEW BUILDING (ENGLAND AND WALES) 1977-1990

Dwellings

Sales   New building

Source: Housing and construction statistics
1. Provisional figures

In 1981, a third of all households in Britain were in council housing. By the end of the decade the figure was nearer 24 per cent. This decline cannot be attributed to council house sales in isolation. High sales have coincided with low and falling levels of public sector new build. Between 1980 and 1981, sales of local authority dwellings in England and Wales outstripped public sector new build for the first time and have done so by a wide margin ever since (Figure 1). In previous periods of high discretionary sales, new building was considerably higher than disposals.

Sales peaked in 1982, and began to decline steadily, prompting some commentators to suggest that the future impact would be limited. By the end of the 1980s, however, sales had risen again to the second highest level of all time, although they fell back substantially in 1990 and have continued to do so.

Against a background of high house prices (and therefore high sales valuations), rising interest rates and a general recession in the owner occupied market, the high levels of council house sales in 1988 and 1989 may seem surprising. This needs to be balanced, however, against the impact of rising real incomes for households in employment, lower levels of unemployment and rising rents.

Moreover, high discounts cushion right to buy purchasers to some degree from rising prices and mortgage interest rates. The uncertain future for council tenants associated with various provisions in the Housing Act 1988 and the Local Government Act 1989 may also have acted as a further incentive to leave the sector. The fall off in sales in 1990 indicates the impact of the continuing recession in the property market combined with rising unemployment, particularly in areas where sales have traditionally been high. Throughout 1990, quarterly sales in all regions fell consistently.

The right to buy is normally associated with the decline of council housing. But the other side of the equation is equally important. Without council house sales, the substantial expansion of home-ownership throughout the 1980s would not have been achieved. In the early 1980s, sales added more to home ownership than new private sector building.

Table 1

REGIONAL PATTERN OF COUNCIL HOUSE SALES 1979-90

	% of stock sold	% of England sales
North (excl. Cumbria)	19.8	6.7
Yorks and Humberside	19.1	9.3
East Midlands	31.7	8.9
Eastern	30.5	13.7
Greater London (incl. GLC)	20.4	14.9
South Eastern (excl. GLC)	33.4	15.1
South West	27.8	8.6
West Midlands	22.4	11.3
North West (inc. Cumbria)	19.1	11.4
England	31.7	
Scotland	20.5	
Wales	27.4	

Source: Department of Environment Statistics; Housing and Construction Statistics; Hansard.
Note: Figures for England as at 1.4.90; Wales and Scotland as at 3.12.90.

And there have been other impacts on the private sector. For example, some tenants who bought their council houses would have bought elsewhere in the private sector if the right to buy had not existed. Some reduction in demand may therefore have resulted elsewhere in the market. Also, right to buy sales have mainly been financed by building society mortgages and this has increased the demand for, and therefore the cost of, borrowing.

When the right to buy was introduced in 1980, there was at least an implicit assumption that the level of sales would be fairly uniform across the country. Although the demand for home-ownership shows slight regional variations, these are not sufficient to suggest that there would be substantial differences in the take-up of the opportunity to buy council houses. It was also assumed that in the absence of political obstruction (recalcitrant Labour councils), pent-up demand for home-ownership would be released everywhere. In practice, however, the pattern has been very different.

For England as a whole, between 1979 and 1990, some 32 per cent of the council stock was sold. Throughout the period, sales continued to be highest in the South and East of England. Moreover, there is no evidence of the slowest sellers catching up. Between 1985 and 1990, the percentage of stock sold rose by the greatest number of percentage points in the Eastern region (15 per cent), the South East (17 per cent), South West (13 per cent) and East Midlands (17 per cent). It rose by the smallest amount in the North West (8 per cent). Lower sales in greater London complicate any simple North/South pattern although increasing sales of flats have occurred in recent years, boosting sales in inner London and Scotland.

In general, rather than smoothing out the tenure structure of Britain, sales have contributed to a greater unevenness. If this were presented as a polarisation, it would mean that the South West, South East (outside greater London), Eastern, East Midlands and Wales were privatising most rapidly — and the gap between these regions and the Northern regions and London was widening. The West Midlands occupies the middle position. In spite of increasing sales since 1988, Scotland remains a low seller.

Council house sales therefore have advanced further in some regions than others. And it is typically in those areas where home ownership was already high that it has grown the most. This becomes more apparent at the local authority level. By September 1989, 178 of the 366 local authorities in England had sold at least 25 per cent of their stock. Sixty three authorities had sold at least 30 per cent.

One consistent feature of the top sellers is that none of them are in the Northern regions. Sales have been most important in the 'shire' districts, where council housing and renting is already limited; where home ownership was already well established, where houses rather than flats predominate in the council stock, and where incomes and employment are generally high.

WHO BUYS COUNCIL HOUSES?

- More affluent, middle aged tenants
- Families with adult children
- In full time work, usually skilled manual or white collar occupations
- Multiple-earner households

Source: Kerr 1988.

Who buys council houses? The picture is now well established. Studies in different regions and localities show a similar pattern related to age, household structure and occupation. Put simply, buyers are drawn disproportionately from households in work, in the middle of the family life cycle, with one or more earners, with two or more adults and in white collar, skilled or semi-skilled occupations.

Put negatively, those who do not buy are the youngest and oldest, the unemployed, female-headed households, lone parent families, and those in the lowest paid and unskilled sectors.

And in most areas, there is a coincidence between those groups with least bargaining power in the labour market and those in the least desirable parts of the council stock — flats and maisonettes and houses on the least popular estates. Those households have least incentive to buy, and least resources to do so.

Another important dimension of the right to buy concerns the value of the assets which are being acquired by individual households. Council house purchasers were to become members of the emerging 'inheritance' economy, with housing equity to pass on to their children and grandchildren. The geographical unevenness of property values has meant inevitably that some people have gained considerably more than others. Sales have been highest in areas of high, and appreciating, property values. In those areas, discounts have been worth most and have been a major incentive to buy. Fewer have bought in the north of the country. There, purchasers have paid less, their discounts were worth less, and absolute increases in property values since purchase have been least. In other words, the generally less affluent North has benefited less than the generally more affluent South.

The development of council house sales policy has not been universally welcomed. The discretionary policies which applied before 1980 were adopted by some Labour local authorities, and were rejected by some Conservative ones. Much of the early controversy about the policy related to the Labour party's opposition, and to what government regarded as obstructive, delaying tactics by some local authorities.

Government's response was not only to tighten legislation, but also to use its powers to pressurise and intervene. Legal challenges to this failed, and the degree of central scrutiny and promotion of policy implementation has been in stark contrast to, say, its approach to homelessness. If this opposition was unsuccessful, that of housing associations was more effective. Government's plans to extend the policy in this area and in relation to dwellings used by elderly and disabled persons were repeatedly thwarted, especially by the House of Lords.

But the controversies about sales are not all about resistance. The degree of centralisation of policy has itself been questioned. The private sector housing industry and housing professions have generally benefited. And the activities of some private sector agencies seeking to generate business through the sales policy have raised controversy. The manipulation of discretionary policies, vacant sales and allocations, notably in Westminster and Wandsworth, are questionable in a number of ways.

The importance of council house sales in governments' public expenditure plans has been apparent ever since 1979. Capital receipts from the housing programme have been more important than the headline-catching sales of state-owned enterprises. Only from 1984/85 onwards have *non-housing* capital receipts exceeded housing receipts in any one year.

For the period of 1979-89, capital receipts for the housing programme were £17.58 billion compared with £23.479 billion from all other privatisations. Housing receipts represented 43 per cent of all privatisation proceeds.

Just as important, they have provided a continuing stream of receipts, rather than a short-lived windfall, and have been an important element in public expenditure planning. The

Table 2

CAPITAL RECEIPTS FROM HOUSING AND OTHER PRIVATISATION PROGRAMMES, 1979-89 (£ million)

	Housing Total	Local Authorities	Other
1979/80	472	448	377
1980/81	603	568	405
1981/82	1045	976	493
1982/83	1877	1739	488
1983/84	1958	1761	1139
1984/85	1804	1628	2171
1985/86	1787	1617	2707
1986/87	2132	1899	4460
1987/88	2462	2190	5139
1988/89 (est)	3440	3150	6100

Source: Cmnd 9428-11 and Cm 609.

implications for taxation and borrowing of any given level of expenditure are reduced if there are capital receipts against which it can be offset. The housing programme made a considerable contribution to reductions in the overall Public Sector Borrowing Requirement and to public sector debt repayment.

In the period since 1979, the large receipts accruing to the housing programme have not been used to boost housing investment. New local authority capital expenditure has declined to a negligible level, and was planned to become negative by 1989/90. There is no doubt that if the local authority housing programme is treated as self-contained, the term 'asset stripping' is perfectly appropriate.

The same process, on a much smaller scale, has been occurring in new towns. Their net capital expenditure has been negative since 1984/85. Receipts have been used to reduce net expenditure. Moreover, until 1991, capital receipts from housing regularly over-achieved because of rising house prices, the increased share of private financing of sales and the increased level of sales.

Losers from the process of council house sales are much less directly identifiable than gainers. As the council sector is reshaped, it provides less housing, less choice and less variety in type and quality. Those who cannot, or do not want, to buy will wait longer for a property, especially for a house rather than a flat, or a transfer. Some of this involves waiting longer in temporary housing, and being homeless longer.

It is not accurate to argue, though, that every council house sold has an immediate impact on someone else's housing opportunities. Sales of vacant council dwellings do have an immediate impact. Who benefits from such sales depends on price and eligibility, but purchasers differ from those who would have been allocated to such dwellings had they been relet. However, the impact of sales to sitting tenants is different. Most sitting tenant purchasers would not have moved out of their homes if they had not bought — so sales do not initially reduce the number of dwellings available for letting. But when their occupiers do move, there is a change in who can take advantage of the ensuing vacancy.

At that stage, the situation is the same as for vacant dwelling sales. Especially in higher house price areas, the household which would have been allocated the property as a council tenant is unlikely to be a potential open market purchaser. The loss of relets does rebound on the same households affected by affordability issues generally, and those most at risk of being homeless. This loss is cumulative, and by 1991 is well in excess of the level of new building in the public sector.

The loss of relets will be greatest where sales have been highest and home ownership has grown most rapidly. This is often in areas where the opportunities for those seeking and needing to rent were already most limited. Indeed, there is a close relationship between high selling areas, and areas where major problems of affordability have developed.

High sales, and limited new build, have had a noticeable effect on the public sector dwelling stock. The selective nature of sales, combined with limited new build, has led to a decline in the proportion of the stock made up of three-bedroomed houses, and a parallel increase in smaller dwellings and flats. Arun, the highest seller at September 1989, had sold almost 40 per cent of its stock. In 1979, 56 per cent of its stock consisted of three-bedroomed dwellings. In 1989, the figure was 36.8 per cent. Bromley, another high seller, shows a reduction of 20 per cent.

Flats have become more numerically significant and there has been a sharp reduction in the percentage of houses. What this means is that those who remain in council housing are now more likely to be living in flats or bungalows, and those households on the waiting list are less likely to be offered a house. A greater contrast between home ownership and council housing has therefore emerged in terms of dwelling type. Council housing is slowly but surely becoming a sector of flats and old persons' dwellings.

Questions about what has been done with the proceeds of sales, and about the declining choices and opportunities of those unable to buy in the housing market, take the discussion back to council house sales as part of the general reshaping of housing policy. There has been an explicit rejection of methods of planning to meet housing need. Sales have been encouraged alongside a planned reduction in local authority building. The aim has been to create a climate in which the private sector would take the lead, and in which direct state provision would be unnecessary.

This policy experiment has failed, as the volatility of the private market has led to reduced building just when public sector building is at a new low, and when affordability and homelessness problems are most striking. Moreover, the policy took no account of the impact of increased social polarisation or of the process of residualisation of council housing.

Residualisation refers to the increasing concentration of lower income groups, the unemployed and those dependent on welfare benefits in particular parts of the housing market. Council house sales have added to and complicated this process of residualisation, but they have not caused it. The process was well under way in the 1960s — before mass sales occurred. It is the decline in low priced privately rented housing which is the most important housing change. Lower income households who previously had been concentrated in this sector have been

150 *Built to last*

forced to look elsewhere. They cannot afford to buy, and have become increasingly concentrated in the social rented sector.

What will happen to the sale of council houses in the 1990s? In 1991, sales had already fallen sharply from the 1990 level. One lesson to learn from the past decade is not to underestimate the possibility of substantial change occurring in housing provision. Different political scenarios offer different likely directions for public housing and housing policy.

The current Conservative government has promised further attempts to reduce the role of the council sector, and to change the tenure status of those who remain in council housing. Peter Walker's idea of transforming rents into mortgage payments has emerged in rent-to-mortgage schemes introduced in Scotland, Wales and selected areas in England. Take-up has, however, been low and the impact is unlikely to be dramatic, but the schemes will be introduced more widely over the next couple of years.

One reason why other privatisation initiatives have not had the impact of the right to buy is that the government believed its own propaganda. The popularity of the right to buy was confused with the unpopularity of council housing. With the right to buy, some tenants recognised a good deal when they saw it. There was not, however, a mass desire to leave the council sector regardless of the destination. There may be widespread problems in the council sector, but there is little evidence that tenants believe that private landlords could do a better job. The original justification for the right to buy was the evidence that a large number of public tenants wanted to become home owners. This is a far cry from offering alternative landlords, or the restructuring of financial regimes to encourage more tenants, in a position to do so, to leave the sector.

Over the next ten years, the right to buy is likely to continue to erode the council stock. Higher rents will fuel this. At the same time higher rents, continuing limitations on local authority capital expenditure and the impact of the right to buy itself may encourage more authorities to undertake voluntary transfers of stock. These will be designed to provide a shelter against the right to buy and keep a social rented sector intact. Existing tenants will keep the right to buy under such transfers, but new

KEY LEGISLATION ON THE RIGHT TO BUY

PRE 1980
- discretionary powers available to local authorities to sell council dwellings

HOUSING ACT 1980
- introduces statutory right to buy for all secure tenants (most tenants)
- statutory procedure for implementation
- discount linked to length of tenancy, 33 per cent for three years tenancy rising by one per cent per year up to maximum of 50 per cent
- right to a mortgage from the local authority

HOUSING AND BUILDING CONTROL ACT 1984
- tightens up original RTB legislation
- extends scope of RTB to more tenants
- eligible to buy after two years tenancy
- minimum discount 32 per cent rising to 60 per cent

HOUSING AND PLANNING ACT 1986
- increases discounts on flats, 44 per cent after two years tenancy rising by two per cent per year to a maximum of 70 per cent
- period for discount repayment reduced from five years to two

HOUSING ACT 1988
- further tightening of RTB legislation
- further development of broader based approach to privatisation of council estates, housing action trusts, change of landlord scheme

tenants will have assured status without the right to buy, and will be faced with higher rents than their neighbours.

What happens to the council sector is also intimately connected to what happens in the housing market and the economy more generally. The level of mortgage interest rates, trends in real incomes, trends in employment and the geography of economic growth and decline in the 1990s will all affect developments in home ownership and the housing opportunities of different groups.

In terms of the growth of home ownership and the important fiscal impact of the right to buy, there can certainly be no re-run of the 1980s. Council housing is a finite resource and a substantial proportion of the best assets have already been bought by those with the resources to do so.

We may expect a continuing stream of sales to sitting tenants in the 1990s, but they are unlikely to be sustained at the level they have achieved in the last decade. Moreover, only now are the consequences of the one dimensional nature of British housing policy which dominated much of the 1980s beginning to emerge.

Housing policy is in disarray. Homelessness has become a political embarrassment. Mortgage arrears have increased dramatically, and repossessions have reached crisis proportions for the financial institutions as well as the households involved. Major affordability problems have developed, especially in the pressurised housing markets of southern England. The right to buy has had a critical impact on the capacity of rural authorities to provide for local needs. The privately rented sector shows little sign of a significant revival. Housing starts in the private sector have continued to decline. The voluntary sector does not offer the immediate prospect of filling the gap left by the lack of new building in the council sector. It is an obvious irony that problems of a shortage of rented housing have begun to be identified and have been a major factor in voluntary transfers.

There are relatively long time lags in housing between policy change and policy consequence. Whatever may be the shape or political complexion of the governments of the 1990s, there will be important consequences of the right to buy sales of the 1980s. An important dimension of these long term changes is the resale of former council dwellings. By 1993 almost two million dwellings will have been transferred from the public to the private sector under the right to buy and other schemes. As those properties filter into the private market, the role and social composition of some council estates will begin to change.

Large tracts of housing and land will become subject to market processes. In the past, the 'zones of transition' were typically areas of inner city private renting which were being transformed, by tenure transfers, into home ownership. In the next decade, such changes may be more closely associated with the inner and outer suburbs. Council housing is not a uniform product and the market will assimilate former council dwellings in different ways. Some estates are more identifiably 'council' than others. Some will have a much higher value than others. We may not see the gentrification of former council estates, but we will certainly see the occupancy of former council dwellings dictated by ability to pay. And entry costs will be much higher in some places than in others.

Any long term assessment of the right to buy would have to acknowledge its significant social, political and fiscal impact. In many ways council house sales set the tone for policy changes in other spheres and the right to buy will always be seen as one of the major policies of the Thatcher governments. Without the right to buy, a substantial number of working class households could not have gained access to home ownership. And of course, without council housing, there could have been no right to buy. But a broader assessment would also have to acknowledge the consequences for those on the outside looking in.

We have not yet seen the end of council housing, and if the next generation is to enjoy the same opportunities of access to good housing and home ownership, substantial new investment will be required. There is certainly no evidence that the contraction of council housing has created opportunities which private sector institutions are able and willing to fill. Something more has to happen on the private side or problems of homelessness and declining standards of housing will become more widespread. The need for a renewed and continuing programme of social rented housing both to offset these problems, and to maintain the right to buy route to home-ownership, is paramount.

(This article was first published in ROOF, September 1990, and updated in December 1991).

Chapter 18

From the poor law to the marketplace

The history of welfare services for elderly people offers lessons to the current plans for housing and community care provision.

Robin Means

Caring for people, the White Paper on community care, and the subsequent NHS and Community Care Act 1990, called for social services to be given the lead role in community care. This did not imply that they should be monopoly service providers, but rather that they should maximise service delivery by the independent sector. As such, these changes are part of the general trend in the welfare state towards what Le Grand[1] calls 'quasi markets' — attempts to develop elements of competition in such diverse areas as health care, education, social rented housing and community care.

The community care changes have major implications for housing policy and housing agencies. Firstly, the White Paper emphasises the need to enable all the 'community care' groups to live in ordinary housing rather than institutions.

Secondly, it recognises the importance of high quality, appropriate housing as an essential component of any community care strategy, and calls upon social services departments 'to work closely with housing authorities, housing associations and other providers of housing of all types in developing plans for a full and flexible range of housing'. This includes not just a limited amount of specialist accommodation, but *all* housing provision, including the repair and maintenance problems of elderly owner occupiers.

Thirdly, social services departments will be expected increasingly to contract out their social care activities to a variety of service providers. Housing agencies may become major service providers, not just of specialist housing services (sheltered accommodation, hostels and home improvement agencies) but also through expanding their role into providing domiciliary services (home care, meals on wheels), or taking over the management of residential homes.

Hulton Deutsch

Corridor in the Highbury Hall home for elderly people in Birmingham, 1949.

Overall, the White Paper argues that all the community care groups should be a high priority for resources, and that flexible care packages can allow most people to live in ordinary housing rather than institutions. It also says that the voluntary sector has the capacity to play a lead role in service provision. These three assumptions have always been at the centre of debates about social care and elderly people.

The origins of many social care services can be traced back to the Second World War. In the first half of the war, sick and frail elderly people were often defined as a problem. If they stayed in the community, they placed pressure on women needed in the munitions factories or they 'cluttered up' public air raid shelters. If they went into hospitals or public assistance institutions, they blocked beds which the authorities wanted to reserve for war casualties.

They tended to be a low priority for evacuation from areas threatened with bomb damage. When the evacuation division of the Ministry of Health considered removal of elderly people from London institutions, it decided 'babies and expectant mothers clearly have first claim and the infirm or aged equally clearly last claim'.[2]

Such attitudes softened as the war progressed. The Beveridge Report was concerned with developing social security arrangements *after* the war, but it was also concerned with maintaining civilian morale by offering a vision of reconstructed post-war Britain.

For example, concern about morale was a major factor in the extension of the maternity-based home help services to elderly people. Both the Ministry of Health and the Ministry of Labour expressed concern in the mid-1940s at 'the hardship which is arising owing to the lack of domestic help in private households where there is sickness or where there are aged or infirm persons and the deleterious effects which this may have on service and civilian morale'.

The extension of the home help service to influenza-hit households and those with frail or sick elderly inhabitants in December 1944 reflected the desire to avoid both the compassionate leave for service staff and the absenteeism amongst women munitions workers which had occurred the previous winter.

Mobile meals services can be traced back to 1943. Their rationale was that frail and sick elderly people found it difficult to queue for food rations. The Ministry of Health initially showed little interest in these schemes. However, early 1947 saw a spate of newspaper stories about food rationing and elderly people ('How are the old folk on the rations?', *Daily Express*; 'Many Leeds Aged on Brink of Starvation', *Yorkshire Evening News*). This led to a flurry of activity, with the Ministry of Health urging voluntary organisations to develop such schemes as soon as possible.

But it was in residential care that the biggest changes occurred. The remnants of the poor law and the workhouse hung over public assistance institutions (PAIs). Residents were frequently not allowed to wear their own clothes, there were restrictions on going out, and all rights to pensions had to be given up unless entry was because of illness and not frailty.

For the majority of elderly people, such institutions were held in abhorrence so that, as Titmuss put it 'the fear of being treated as a pauper was much more real than the fear of bombs.'[3]

However, disruption caused by the war was sucking elderly people who would have normally avoided such care into public assistance institutions, and they ended up in large institutions short of staff, food and other facilities as a result of the war effort.

Some elderly people made homeless by bomb damage were placed in small homeless hostels where pension rights were retained, but a clear line between war victims and ordinary PAI cases was hard to maintain.

In March 1943 a journalist from the *Manchester Guardian* visited a workhouse and spoke of 'a frail, sensitive, refined old woman' of 84 who was forced to live in the following regime:

'Down each side of the ward were ten beds, facing one another. Between each bed and its neighbour was a small locker and a straight-backed, wooden, uncushioned chair. On each chair sat an old woman in workhouse dress, upright, unoccupied. No library books or wireless. Central heating, but no open fire. No easy chairs. No pictures on the walls . . . There were three exceptions to the upright old women. None was allowed to lie on her bed at any time throughout the day, although breakfast is at 7 am, but these three, unable any longer to endure their physical and mental weariness, had crashed forward, face downwards, on to their immaculate bedspreads and were asleep.'

This article had the effect of speeding up pressure for change. The Ministry of Health received a growing pile of complaints from pressure groups, local authority associations and professional associations about inadequate hospital and residential provision for elderly people. Civil servants admitted the inadequacies, but claimed the war had undermined attempts at reform.

Further embarrassment was caused by the profile of PAIs painted by *Old people*,[4] the 1947 Survey Committee which was chaired by B S Rowntree and funded by the Nuffield Foundation. In a 1947 circular, the Ministry of Health called for the opening of smaller homes, and for larger homes to relax rules on visiting, clothing, private lockers and clocking in and out.

The main focus of the 1948 National Assistance Act was to sort out public assistance institutions to avoid future scandals.

Section 21 of the Act said that: 'It should be the duty of every
local authority . . . to provide residential accommodation for
persons who by reasons of age, infirmity or any other
circumstances are in need of care and attention which is not
otherwise available to them'. Such homes were expected to be
smaller and more homely than PAIs, and residents would pay
for their accommodation and maintenance.

The 1948 Act showed little enthusiasm for encouraging the
growth of domiciliary services. Local authorities were given no
general power to promote the welfare of elderly people. They
were not allowed to develop their own meals on wheels services
and luncheon clubs, although they could give grants to
voluntary agencies. Section 29 limited the general powers of
local authorities to develop services to those who were 'blind,
deaf and dumb and other persons who were substantially and
permanently handicapped by illness, injury or congenital
deformity'. However, the 1946 National Health Service Act had
given local authorities the power to develop home help services
for a range of groups including 'the aged'.

The reasons for this heavy emphasis upon residential care
and neglect of domiciliary services are complex. One reason
was that the priority was to tackle the problem of large,
outdated, PAIs. However, an equally important factor was a
belief that support in the home should only be offered by
relatives or voluntary workers.

During the Second World War, voluntary organisations, such
as the British Red Cross Society, NOPWC (now Age Concern)
and the Women's Royal Voluntary Service, developed a range
of services such as small residential homes, meals on wheels,
day centres and visiting schemes. They were keen to further
develop their role further after 1948.

Such aspirations received strong back-up from senior officials
at the Ministry of Health. They were pessimistic about the
potential of domiciliary services to stop elderly people entering
residential care. At best, they were an extra frill to be provided
by voluntary organisations for the lonely and temporarily ill who
lacked family support. Any attempt to challenge this view was
attacked.

In 1948/49, Labour authorities like Liverpool, York and
Blackburn, were pressing for permission to establish services

for elderly people in their own homes, especially visiting schemes. In April 1949, Barbara Castle (MP for Blackburn) asked Minister of Health Aneurin Bevan if the 1948 Act could be used to legalise the establishment of such services and he agreed to look at this. But public record office files show that the civil servants were determined to undermine such aspirations.

The key assistant secretary in the Ministry of Health remained convinced 'the job is essentially one for voluntary rather than local authority effort' and a circular on the 'Welfare of Old People' argued that the experience gained since the 1948 Act: 'Has shown an urgent need for further services of the more personal kind which are not covered by existing statutory provision and which indeed are probably best provided by voluntary workers activated by a spirit of good neighbourliness.' Local old people's welfare committees were asked to co-ordinate such effort. This circular is often described as representing a liberalisation of government policy when really it was an attempt to ensure local authorities remained focused narrowly upon the provision of residential care.

The emphasis upon residential care was soon abandoned. The 1954 annual report of the Ministry of Health claimed 'the importance of enabling old people to go on living in their own homes where they most wish to be, and of delaying admission to residential care for as long as possible is now generally accepted'. A 1954 political pamphlet for the Conservative Political Centre agreed that 'we should devote all our energies to enabling old people to continue living in their own homes'.[5]

In addition, faith in residential provision by local authorities backed up by domiciliary provision, mainly provided by voluntary organisations, was soon challenged. *The last refuge*[6] by Peter Townsend was published in the early 1960s and provided a damning indictment of local authority residential care. He claimed all such homes (former PAIs, old converted houses and new purpose built homes) offered a poor quality of life because all institutions undermined independence and residents failed to make new friendships. Nearly all residents could remain in the community with proper pensions, good domiciliary services and more sheltered housing.

His most damning comments were reserved for the large former PAIs. Townsend visited 39 such institutions and found that 57 per cent of the accommodation was in rooms with at least ten beds. Many of the staff had initially been employed under the poor law system and had received no retraining. He found that a minority of them 'were unsuitable, by any standards, for the tasks they performed, men or women with authoritarian attitudes inherited from poor law days who provoked resentment and even terror among infirm people'.

At the same time, local authorities were becoming frustrated at the failure of voluntary organisations to develop coherent authority-wide services in areas such as meals on wheels, day care and visiting/counselling schemes. This created what one commentator called a 'wind of discontent in the town halls'.[7] Voluntary organisations such as NOPWC and WRVS were tending to argue amongst themselves about how to co-ordinate their services. Volunteer availability was varied, with recruitment often easiest in areas with the least need. Services were not only patchy but where they existed they often ran for only a few days a week and closed during school holidays.

This situation was confirmed for meals services by a 1960 survey carried out by Amelia Harris for the National Corporation for the Care of Old People (now the Centre for Policy on Ageing). The chair of that organisation concluded that 'the scale on which this service should be provided to meet all needs is beyond the scope of voluntary finance and their resources of manpower: and it is clear that the time had come when authorities, in spite of the ever increasing demand on them, should become responsible for this important service.'[8]

Despite the, apparently, almost universal enthusiasm for care at home, and despite evidence of the failure of local authority residential care and voluntary provided domiciliary services, policy and legislative changes were slow to emerge. The 1960s and early 1970s were boom years for the building of new local authority residential homes.

The full legal powers for local authorities to provide domiciliary services for elderly people (other than home care) did not occur until the early 1970s. A 1962 amendment of the 1948 National Assistance Act enabled local authorities to provide their own meals on wheels services. The 1968 Public

Health Services and Public Health Act gave local authorities the general power to promote the welfare of elderly people, and the 1970 Chronically Sick and Disabled Persons Act placed a further set of obligations on local authorities (assessment for telephones, home adaptations) although the implementation of these last acts was delayed to coincide with the creation of unified social services departments in April 1971. Previously, personal social services for children, elderly people and most of the community care groups were provided by a variety of small local authority departments.

The pace of change was slow. Much of the Ministry of Health comment about staying at home may have been mere rhetoric, hiding a continued belief that the state should concentrate upon residential care while the family and voluntary organisations should help people stay at home. Townsend has argued that the expensive provision of residential care for a minority helps to mask the lack of commitment through pensions and other services for the majority.

Certainly, through much of the 1950s and early 1960s, many believed that a major growth of state provided domiciliary services would undermine the willingness of women to go on caring for frail and dependent parents and parents-in-law. The Association of Municipal Corporations, in their evidence to the 1954 Phillips Committee on the economic and financial problems of old age, spoke of 'the reluctance of many families to care for their aged relatives'. In 1959, the chief welfare officer of Manchester was lamenting the 'changed attitude towards aged dependants' while a colleague was warning that 'it would be an administrative nightmare if there was a decline in family responsibility'.

Such attitudes were especially strong within the health service with its concern to avoid the unnecessary blocking of beds. As a consultant physician from a Southampton geriatric unit explained in 1958:

'The feeling that the State ought to solve every inconvenient domestic situation is merely another factor in producing a snowball expansion of demands in the National Health (and Welfare) Services. Close observation on domestic strains makes one thing very clear. This is that where an old person has a family who have a sound feeling of moral responsibility, serious problems do not arise, however much difficulty may be met.'

Such views posed two questions. Did the 'family' still accept its responsibilities towards elderly parents? And did state supported services support or undermine the 'family' in this respect?

Gradually, overwhelming evidence accumulated that wives, daughters and daughters-in-law continued to provide the majority of care for frail and dependent elderly people. An early 1960s study of 1,500 patients discharged from a geriatric unit in Edinburgh illustrated the willingness of relatives to support home care and led the researchers to conclude that 'the belief in the decline in filial care of the elderly is unfounded and an as yet unproven modern myth'.[9]

Such conclusions were supported by a series of studies involving Peter Townsend, the largest of which entailed 4,000 interviews with elderly people in three different industrialised counties and recommended that rather than being restricted from a fear of undermining the family, domiciliary services needed to be expanded rapidly to support families and help the isolated.

Sadly, despite the legislation of the late 1960s and the creation of social services departments in April 1971, no great 'take-off' took place in the provision of flexible, home-based services for elderly people. Most resources continued to go on residential care, while senior managers and qualified social workers devoted the vast majority of their energy towards families 'at risk', especially after the death of young Maria Colwell in January 1973, which was blamed upon the failure of social workers to intervene effectively.

This brief history of the development of welfare services for elderly people since the Second World War and through to April 1971 has illustrated a number of points of relevance to housing workers and housing agencies. First, the full legislative empowerment of local authorities has been quite recent and, therefore, it is perhaps not surprising how little thought has been given to the housing dimension of community care. But the bombing raids of the Second World War provided an excellent illustration of how housing problems ensure elderly people drift into institutional care. Policy makers in that period massively overestimated civilian injuries, but failed to comprehend the likely extent of home damage, and its consequences for groups such as elderly people.

It seems we have learnt very little, since there is a continued failure to develop complementary social care and housing policies. Statements in the 1990 White Paper about the importance of good quality housing to community care strategies will mean nothing so long as mainstream housing policies ensure such housing is increasingly not available to elderly people on low incomes.

Secondly, we can see how the voluntary sector has been given a pivotal role in service provision on a previous occasion, and that this was taken away because of its failure to develop sufficiently coherent patterns of service. Will the same problems occur in the 1990s, or will social services departments learn to operate a contract economy to ensure the provision of flexible high quality services? This may be interpreted as the need to squeeze costs (the cheapest tender wins), rather than a concern to ensure that good voluntary organisations do not lose their ability to innovate and invest in organisation development.

On the other hand, large voluntary organisations which obtain monopoly service contracts in a particular area may find themselves in a position where the local authority is not able to purchase from an alternative supplier even if their performance turns out to be unsatisfactory. It is far from clear whether consumers will gain or lose from these major changes.[10]

Finally, the history of welfare services for elderly people warns that it is always a struggle to ensure that these services gain the same level of priority as child care. The full implementation of the community care reforms has been delayed and our television screens are filled with stories about social workers and child sexual abuse (Cleveland, Rochdale and the Orkneys). Are social services departments going to lose interest in elderly people and community care once again?

Notes

1. J. Le Grand (1990) *Quasi-markets and social policy*, SAUS, University of Bristol.
2. Quoted in R Means and R Smith, *The development of welfare services for elderly people*, (1985) Croom Helm. All quotations in this article can be found in this book unless reference separately.
3. R Titmuss, *Problems of social policy*, (1976 edition) HMSO.

4. B S Rowntree, *Old people: report of a survey committee*, (1980 edition) Arno Press.
5. J Vaughan-Morgan, A Maude and K Thompson, *The care of old people*, (1952) Conservative Political Centre.
6. P Townsend, *The last refuge*, (1964 edition) Routledge.
7. K Slack, *Councils, committees and concern for the old*, (1960) Codicote Press.
8. Foreword to A Harris, *Meals on wheels for old people*, (1986) NCCOP.
9. C Lowther and J Williamson, 'Old People and Their Relatives', *The Lancet*, 31 December 1986.
10. L Hoyes and R Means, *Implementing The White Paper on community care*, School for Advanced Urban Studies, University of Bristol, 1991.

(This article was first published in ROOF, May 1991).

Chapter 19

Hindsight

A sense of perspective on the history of housing is only valuable if it stimulates the foresight to develop better housing policies.

Peter Williams

The series of articles in this book reminds us of the complex and contentious history of housing policy and practice in the UK. It cautions against those who claim instant and universal solutions to housing problems. The series has also highlighted certain themes and continuities in the long running saga of the housing question in Britain. These include the role of protest by individuals and groups, the contested history of council housing, the battle over subsidies for people or property, and the continuing failure to meet housing needs and to remove discrimination.

A 'second take' allows us all the privilege of hindsight, an ability much in evidence in housing but insufficiently used when it comes to shaping housing policy. At the time of writing, we have two 'second take' ministers at the Department of the Environment, Michael Howard and Sir George Young. Both have had an opportunity to take stock, and consider the strengths and weaknesses of policy. To get the parcel twice (or, in the case of Sir George Young, three times) when the music stops may be regarded by some as very bad luck. It ought to mean better and clearer understanding of the housing problems facing us.

Surrounded by reports and manifestos, bombarded by invitations to attend seminars and conferences, it can be hard to fully appreciate the role that ordinary people have played in the development of policy, often through direct action. Indeed, perhaps the notion of direct action itself has faded in the last decade, despite the profile given to consumer rights. It still exists, though it may often be exercised individually, rather than collectively. The votes against the early housing action trusts are an example of this. The rent strikes of the early 1900s and in the 1970s, the surcharging of councillors, and most recently the mass non-payment of community charge tell us that people continue to mount mass protest and achieve change.

At the same time, protest and pressure have become more structured and organised. Arguments are researched and reports presented. Facts as well as emotions are delivered. Sadly, while the case for change is better presented than ever before, government has shown considerable ability in ignoring the evidence. Through a smokescreen of minor policy responses and counter-attacks, typically on local government, existing policies tend to roll forward. For those seeking change, and for those experiencing the negative consequences of policy, the importance of direct action cannot be ignored. The debate must not take place simply between experts at a national level.

The 1992 general election offered the opportunity for a real 'test of opinion', but housing was not a high profile issue. Yet although most people are reasonably housed in a physical sense, many find the costs of housing too high, and many have no home at all. And the indirect costs arising from the deficiencies of the UK housing system impose major expenditure burdens on central and local government, as well on individual households.

The recognition of the importance of choice, and the need for variety, has not undermined the case for council housing. All the evidence points towards the sound logic for a well-organised and properly-funded public sector. We cannot disregard the contribution that council housing has made to the improvement of housing standards and to the wellbeing of millions of individual families. At the same time, it is clear from the accounts in this book that there was no inevitable and pre-ordained case for council housing. Like any initiative, its origins are a combination of politics, necessity, and chance.

Council housing has always been contentious — it has had an uneasy past, and has an uncertain future. If the case for a public sector can be made, how big should it be? With home-ownership now the major tenure, council housing will provide for the minority, along with housing associations and other private landlords.

There is now a general recognition that with appropriate safeguards and standards, the private landlord has a role to play in certain segments of the market. Private renting should be promoted as an alternative to home ownership, and it is here that its future lies. It cannot be considered as an alternative to the public sector.

The current government has been keen to distiguish today's private landlord from those of previous eras. This is difficult to achieve without considerable regulation, and works against a large and vibrant sector. The move towards market rents may blur distinctions and expand opportunities, but the tension between needs, rents and profits remains.

Housing associations, like private landlords, have been promoted as an important alternative to councils. But their history suggests a need for caution about their true capacity to replace the council landlord. A commitment to local communities, and to a 'small scale' approach, works against the creation of large national organisations. Economic pressures, competition and ambition will continue to force associations away from their origins, although some are trying to preserve their local role.

Throughout this century, there has been a continuing revolution in the role and meaning of specific tenures. Private renting was replaced by council housing and home ownership. Now council housing is being squeezed by home ownership and housing association provision. Housing associations and home ownership are also under pressure from a revived rented sector (which might include arms length rental companies formed by local authorities). The process of change is continuous and dynamic.

If the history of council housing is contentious, so too is the question of how we finance housing. Do we reduce the cost of buying or renting a home by subsidising the building, or do we subsidise individuals to allow them to pay the price the market dictates? The history of housing finance, as revealed in this book, is one of a long and hard fought campaign for supremacy between these two different perspectives.

Currently, it is the second approach that is winning — building subsidies have been cut while housing benefit has 'taken the strain'. But housing benefit is no universal solution. There are major problems of assessment and exclusion, of the rate at which benefit is withdrawn as income rises, and of the creation of poverty traps. As the deficiencies emerge, the case for subsidies to property rather than people is reasserting itself.

Local councils and associations are now locked into finance systems which force rents up. The opportunity to exercise local discretion has been reduced, creating a conflict between rent levels and local needs. Central control over rents is now greater than ever, even though all housing organisations are being asked to be more responsive to their local communities.

Higher rents blur the contrast between renting and buying, but the current levels of mortgage and rent arrears demonstrate the problems many people face in meeting their housing costs. In some cases this is a temporary problem, caused by short-time working or unemployment, but for others it is a clash between income and outgoings in which housing costs loom large. The upward pressures on housing costs and the loss of local discretion puts the focus and responsibility directly back onto central government.

Local and central government involvement in housing has emerged slowly over the century. Local government's initial reluctance to get involved in housing gradually changed as subsidy increased and the local electoral appeal of housing provision developed. Central government took an enabling role, supporting and guiding local government, but not directing it. Now, it is local authorities who must, according to central government, be enablers and not providers.

The tension between central and local government is not new, and there will inevitably be friction between two layers of government. But in the last 13 years, the conflicts have reached new heights. From the centre, local government is viewed as being a very imperfect mechanism for delivering centrally-determined policy; at the local level, regardless of party affiliation, central government is seen as seizing every opportunity to reduce the scope of local government.

The battle is not easily resolved, and the cost is not borne by the protagonists, but by local residents, the ordinary people that both sides would argue they are serving. Because housing is such an important local function, the sooner the conflict can be resolved, the better for all concerned.

The evidence on who bears the cost of inadequate housing has been plain for years. Discrimination against minority groups reflecting factors like race, class or household type has been evident in the housing system, whether in local authority housing, the private rented sector or home ownership. The history of the homelessness legislation highlights the view about 'deserving' and 'undeserving' cases.

Securing appropriate housing to meet the diversity of needs remains a problem. Voluntary provision has long been encouraged to grow up around the edges of what may be seen as the core providers, the local authorities. This was how housing associations were promoted in the 1970s, and today similar expectations are being placed on the voluntary sector with regard to community care.

This raises major questions about co-ordination between providers, their competence and commitment, and the resources available. There is merit in encouraging diversity, and promoting agencies other than local government to take up these different challenges, but this is a long term process and one in which substantial safeguards must be put into place. The evidence on community care so far is that the emerging system has fundamental weaknesses.

A long term perspective is essential to understand the consequences of housing policy and practice. We need to research and assess problems, to take an overview based on all the available evidence, rather than draw conclusions on the basis of a simple one-off exercise. We have to accept that often, we do not have a full grasp of the housing system and the complex interactions between its different parts.

With hindsight, this is the foresight which is now required. In a recent article,[1] a senior civil servant involved in the 1977 Housing Policy Review reflected on what had not been foreseen and what might be done to prevent it re-occurring. He stressed the need to look over 'the other side of the hill', to anticipate and forecast outcomes and to look for long term gains as distinct from short term expediencies. He pointed to the need to recognise the interconnections and interdependencies between the housing system and other aspects of the economy and society, and stressed the value of independent debate and scrutiny.

Equipped with such virtues, ministers might more readily concede a place for the well-run council housing service and recognise the merits of local authorities playing active and competitive roles in local housing markets. They might also recognise the need to allow time for initiatives to develop fully.

Within this perspective, the case for experimentation and for pilot programmes should be much more fully embraced than at present. There are a number of different ways of tackling specific housing problems. There are also a variety of different contexts in which the same problem arises. Pilot schemes can be an effective way of exploring how best to move policy and practice forward.

This book emphasises the politics of housing policy. It is inconceivable that housing can be depoliticised. At the same time, it is possible to imagine a greater consensus on how to achieve the shared goals of a decent home at a price people can afford. At the end of the day, the policy analysts, the housing professionals and the politicians all have homes to go to. The experts can indulge in the luxury of a 'second take' but it can really only be justified if they learn from it, and if those who need homes benefit in the end.

Notes

1. A Holmans *The 1977 National Housing Policy Review in retrospect*, Housing Studies, vol 6, no. 3, (1991) pp.206-219.

(This article was specially written for inclusion in this book in April 1992).

Suggestions for further reading

Audit Commission, *Housing the Homeless: The Local Authority Role* (1989)

M Boddy, *The Building Societies* (Macmillan, 1980)

M Boleat, *The Building Societies Industry* (Allen and Unwin, 1986)

M Brion and A Tinker, *Women in Housing — Access and Influence* (Housing Centre Trust, 1980)

D Clapham and J English (eds), *Public Housing: Current Trends and Future Developments* (Croom Helm, 1987)

G Darley, *Octavia Hill, A Life* (Constable, 1990)

M Daunton (ed), *Councillors and Tenants: Local Authority Housing in English Cities, 1919-1939* (Leicester University Press, 1984)

Department of the Environment, *The Government's Review of the Homelessness Legislation* (DoE, 1989)

J English (ed), *The Future of Council Housing* (Croom Helm, 1982)

A Evans and S Duncan, *Responding to Homelessness: Local Authority Policy and Practice* (DoE, 1986)

R Forrest and A Murie, *Selling the Welfare State* (Routledge, 1988)

J Greve, D Page, S Greve, *Homelessness in London* (Scottish Academic Press, 1971)

Henderson and Karn, *Race, Class and State Housing* (Gower, 1987)

O Hill, *Homes of the London Poor* (Macmillan 1875, reprinted by Cass, 1970)

A Holmans, *Housing Policy in Britain* (Croom Helm, 1987)

P Kemp (ed), *The Future of Private Renting* (University of Salford, 1988)

P Kemp (ed), *The Private Provision of Rented Housing: Current Trends and Future Prospects* (Avebury, 1988)

P Malpass, *Reshaping Housing Policy: Subsidies, Rents and Residualisation* (Routledge, 1990)

S Merrett, *State Housing in Britain* (Routledge and Kegan Paul, 1979)

A Power, *Property Before People — The Management of Twentieth Century Council Housing* (Allen and Unwin, 1987)

J Rex and S Tomlinson, *Colonial Immigrants in a British City* (Routledge and Kegan Paul, 1979)

J Richards, *The Housing (Homeless Persons) Act 1977: A Study in Policy Making* (Working Paper no. 22, School for Advanced Urban Studies, 1981)

P Sarre et al, *Ethnic Minority Housing: Explanations and Policies* (Avebury, 1989)

S Smith, *The Politics of 'Race' and Residence* (Polity Press, 1989)

M Swenarton, *Homes Fit for Heroes* (Heinemann, 1981)

J White, *Rothschild Buildings* (Routledge, 1980)

A Wohl, *The Eternal Slum* (Edward Arnold, 1977)

Index

Local Government and Housing Act,
  1989, 26, 31, 48, 142
Local Government, Planning and Land
  Act, 1980, 65
London, 2, 5, 6, 9, 27, 85, 86, 104, 112,
  113, 119
London county council, 72

M
MacDonald, R, 44
Macmillan, H, 45, 94, 95
Means testing, 123
Metropolitan Association for Improving
  the Dwellings of the Industrious
  Classes, 2
Middlesbrough, 73
Milner Holland Report, 104, 113
Ministry of Health, 56, 60, 73, 155, 156,
  157, 158, 159, 161
Ministry of Labour, 156
Ministry of Works, 55, 86
Mortgage arrears, 48, 168
Mortgage tax relief, 121

N
Nationality Act, 1948, 101
National Assistance Act, 1948, 129, 157,
  159, 160
National Health Service Act, 1946, 158
New Commonwealth, 101, 104
NHS and Community Care Act, 1990
  154
Notting Hill riots, 1958, 108
Nuffield Foundation, 157

O
Overcrowding, 11, 18, 78, 104, 108
Owen, R, 17
Owner occupation, 46, 57, 94, 96, 98,
  99, 100
Owner occupied sector, 33, 118, 120
Owner occupiers, 29, 44, 58, 77, 113

P
Parker Morris Committee, 1961, 25
Patten, J, 115
Peabody, G, 2, 6
People's house, 94
Phillips Committee, 1954, 161
Powell, E, 109
Philanthropy, 2, 16
Poll tax, 38, 39
Poor Law Amendment Act, 1834, 16

Portal, Lord, 80
Power, A, 23
Prefabrication, 78, 79
Prince Albert, 2
Private landlords, 22, 29, 42, 52, 54, 57,
  74, 104, 110, 111, 167
Private renting, 14, 33, 34, 48, 74, 100,
  103, 104, 110-121, 149, 169
Privatisation, 146, 150
Property owning democracy, 94
Public Assistance Institutions (PAIs)
  156, 157, 160
Public Health Services and Public Health
  Act, 1968, 160-1
Public Sector Borrowing Requirement
  147
Public utility societies, 55

R
Race Relations Act, 1965, 1968, 109
Rachman, P, 113
Rachmanism, 116, 119
Racism, 101, 102
Rate fund contributions, 60, 61, 65
Rate support grant, 65
Rathbone, E, 69, 70
Redbridge, 85, 88, 90
Rent Act, 1957, 110, 111, 112, 120, 121
Rent Act, 1965, 62
Rent allowances, 124
Rent arrears, 18, 38, 168
Rent control, 53, 54, 57, 110, 111
Rent decontrol, 112, 113, 114
Rent deregulation, 116, 117, 118, 120,
  121
Rent officers, 114, 117, 118
Rent pooling, 61, 66
Rent rebates, 63, 67-76, 124
Rents: affordable, 52
  — fair, 62, 114, 123, 124, 125
  — controlled, 113, 123
Rent strikes, 35, 53, 74, 166
Rent-to-mortgage, 150
Residualisation, 93, 98, 99, 149
Ridley, N, 115
Right to buy, 93, 139-153
Ross, S, 133, 134
Rossi, H, 134
Rowntree, BS, 157
Royal Commission on Scottish Housing
  55
Royal Commission on the Housing of the
  Working Classes, 1884-85, 3, 20

You've read the book, now read the magazine . . .

If you don't already get ROOF, you're missing out on Britain's brightest housing magazine.

ROOF is the magazine that:

⁕ brings you the best interviews with the big names in housing — ministers, civil servants, and key figures in the public and private sectors.

⁕ gives the best analysis of new policies with contributors including government ministers, the housing profession, the national media, and the financial and economic worlds.

⁕ puts all the latest housing facts and figures at your fingertips in a useful, at a glance format. (It's no wonder that 85% of ROOF readers use it regularly in their day to day work).

⁕ brought Conservative, Labour and Liberal Democrat housing spokesmen together in the only pre-Election national debate on housing policy, in front of an audience of housing specialists and hosted by broadcaster Nick Ross.

All this, plus regular new updates, legal notes, reviews, and a lively letters column. Take a look at ROOF today and you'll never look back.

ROOF is an editorially independent housing magazine published every two months by Shelter. It is sold on subscription only, with one rate for organisations and a cheaper rate for individual subscribers.

For information on current rates or to take out a subscription, phone ROOF's subscription agents Quadrant on 0444 440421 or write to them at Stuart House, 41-43 Perrymount Road, Haywards Heath, West Sussex, RH16 3BN.